SPECIAL CONDITIONS APPLY

*"A Laymans Exploration of the Romantic
Nuances Of Human Gender"*

"The Instead of Factor"

By
MALCOLM A.J. CHARLES

Order this book online at www.trafford.com
or email orders@trafford.com

Most Trafford titles are also available at major online book retailers.

Note for Librarians: A cataloguing record for this book is available from Library
and Archives Canada at www.collectionscanada.ca/amicus/index-e.html

Printed in Victoria, BC, Canada.

ISBN: 978-1-4269-2575-7 (sc)
ISBN: 978-1-4269-2576-4 (hc)

Library of Congress Control Number: 2010900225

*Our mission is to efficiently provide the world's finest, most comprehensive book publishing
service, enabling every author to experience success. To find out how to publish your book, your
way, and have it available worldwide, visit us online at www.trafford.com*

Trafford rev. 6/22/10

 www.trafford.com

North America & international
toll-free: 1 888 232 4444 (USA & Canada)
phone: 250 383 6864 ♦ fax: 812 355 4082

ACKNOWLEDGEMENTS

(a) To my wife Anita, for her patient attempts at articulating the 'female perspective' earlier on in our relationship, as I sought to cross the "psychological boundaries" of the inner recesses of the feminine mind.

(b) To her niece Anella, for her artistic selection and insertion of the illustrations.

(c) To our family friend, Consultant Physician and Dermatologist, Dr. Marie Grandison-Didier, for her thoughtful and professional insights, as has been input into Chapter #9 of this text.

(d) To my team at the Paramount Marketing Group and to all of my friends and family at home and abroad, for their encouragement and support.

(e) To my yet unknown contributors (via the internet) upon who's reference, I had periodically drawn and to members of my own 'cyberspace circle' around the world, who helped prompt my creative perspectives of positions taken in some of the pages of this Book.

(f)   To my Canada based Publishers, for their tenacity, in steering the production aspects of this work.

LIKE MOST PROFESSIONAL MEN (and women), I have been to "hell and back" where domestic relationships are concerned, all because, I suspect, that unlike academic and professional studies, there is no apparent "School of relationships" akin to "School's of Management", "School's of Medicine", "School's of Accounting", "Engineering, Aeronautics", and the like, where you might 'major' in dealing with the thoughts, perceptions and idiosyncrasies (both male or female), of the opposite gender.

To compound the issue, we men in particular, are somewhat 'averse' to asking for directions and in any event, even knowing who to ask, so we continue to dive off, into a testosterone driven "quicksand of failed relationships".

Never mind the, albeit, apparent 'feminist' notion, that men and women are the same and equal in all respects....

Hello, we are not talking here about 'Fundamental rights at work, based on (ILO) International Labour Standards and other such fun stuff... no, there are fundamental differences in the way males and females perceive the 'romantic component' of our lives; and, the earlier we come, to get to grips and accept that fact, is the earlier we would begin to appreciate how to recognise the potential pitfalls that might beset us along life's journey.

Guys, have you ever observed our ladies in deep conversation, especially if it involves matters of the "opposite" gender??

If you are sufficiently perceptive, you will recognize that there are "non- verbal questions" that we, as men, are far from privy to; but which none the less, sit at the heart of all they are saying; as you will see their heads nodding in agreement, leaving us totally "in the dark" as to what the subject matter is....

The lines of this Book are simply meant to prompt a thought process which would, hopefully, create a greater degree of sensitivity on both sides of the gender divide, and help us examine the various views of both men and women, in our lifelong quest for a greater understanding of this generational mystery; which may avert a situation, as the saying goes, where "many men gain a wife and lose their best friend".

In a nutshell, to be blunt, what men instinctively seem to perceive as simply a (testosterone) driven pursuit of 'horizontal entertainment' (aka "a one night stand"), largely intended as short-term; our female counterparts in contrast, perceive it as the "beginning of a generational genetic process", which will result in a lifelong haul of an exclusive and uninterrupted relationship.

Again for my enlightenment to this interesting phenomenon, which, apparently, comes naturally to the ladies, I give credit to my wife Anita for her painstaking efforts (early in our two decade plus relationship), to explain to my "male" mind and to help answer the 'age old' question, "What is it that women want?"

This question with all of its ramifications has prompted me to continue with my writing hobby, in the form of this Book.

Sincere thanks also are extended to the many MEN, with whom I shared my intentions of penning these lines and who "vowed" to be the "first" to get their copy of my Book; and indeed, those who shared "personal insights" with me which they wanted no one else to know; "especially their wives or lady friends"....

To all of you, I extend my sincerest thanks and appreciation.

Malcolm A.J. Charles

CONTENTS

CHAPTER ONE (1)

Light Hearted Analogy

JUST WHEN YOU THOUGHT you had "mastered the art" of knowing the thoughts and nuances of your spouse, a perspective emerges, that blows your self appointed expertise, "right out of the water!"

You didn't see it coming; you thought you were the man, - "ou pa ne ti bwai encore." (How's my Creole?) You're savvy, smooth, confident, and even seductive..... Sounds familar?

Well, as far as my own research goes, there is yet to be a school, with a curriculum that takes into account, all of the 'variables' that you are likely to encounter in the world of "romantic nuances of human gender".

To start the ball rolling, I came across the following lighthearted "analogy", in my varied research readings on the subject of this work.

Check this one out, as men and women try desperately, to figure out why:-

QUOTE:

• "A man will pay $2 for a $1 item he wants. A woman will pay $1, for a $2 item that she doesn't want!

- A woman worries about the future, until she gets a husband.

- A man never worries about the future, until he gets a wife.

- A successful man is one who makes more money than his wife can spend… A successful woman is one who can find such a man.

- To be happy with a man, you must understand him a lot and love him a little. To be happy with a woman, you must love her a lot, and not try to understand her at all.

- Married men will live longer than single men – but married men, are often, a lot more willing to die.

- Any married man should forget his mistake – there's no use in two people remembering the same thing.

- Men wake up as good-looking as they went to bed. Women, somehow, deteriorate during the night, (am I in trouble yet?)

- A woman marries a man, expecting he will change, but he doesn't. A man on the other hand marries a woman, expecting that she won't change and you know what? - She does.

- A woman has the last word in any argument. Anything a man says after that is the beginning of the new argument.

- There are only 2 times when a man doesn't understand a woman – before marriage and after marriage. Unquote.

No, I am not a clinical psychologist or romance guru -- far from it…have had my own share of ups and downs, mistakes and "boo-boos", like everyone else. And so, the following chapters of this text are merely an observation of what seems to go on between the sexes, which, hopefully, will create greater awareness of ourselves, especially we as men, in what some may call, the "battle of the sexes."

For generations, as far back as I can tell, persons have been crying out for answers to the apparent gender divide, that has been largely responsible for the arguments, fights, psychological warfare, break ups and divorces – even death…

But somehow, the 'experts' on the matter of sex and gender relations, only seem to offer ways of mitigating such conflicts, trying to explain ways of amelioration, reconciliation, tolerance, ability to cope and endure, to the proverbial "till death do us part".

Regrettably, little seems to be asked, as to what might be the right "question".

Why this 'God given' arrangement, for the continuity of the species, often runs into the level of trauma it invariably seems to attract.

What exactly is the cause, or the premise of the cause, of the apparent domestic 'turbulence' which, if we are unable to avert by applying appropriate mitigating techniques, as alluded to above, could very well escalate into a cocktail for disaster.

To my mind, you can never find the "Right Answer" until you begin to ask the question, the right question that is…. but then, what exactly is the "Right Question??"…

One thing is for sure, when the going is good, it is very, very good, but when it is bad, it's an absolute living hell; which I am sure, the best of us, even with a minimal level of experience, will, "under oath", be forced to admit to.

So lets begin together, to travel the journey of a "Laymans Exploration of the Romantic nuances of Human gender perspectives", and hope that someone, somewhere, is helped out of, or at least enabled to avert, the inevitable "sticky situations", that the world of romance, in whatever form you may choose, throws up when you least expect it.

I will sincerely attempt to ask, what could be the basis for the formulating of the questions, but the answers, my dear readers, will be down to you, – as no two situations are exactly alike....

CHAPTER TWO (2)

Contemplations

HAVE YOU EVER STOPPED to try and understand, "What makes men 'tick' but yet makes women 'sick'?" - have you ever figured out, what is the fundamental cause of perceived incompatibility between the sexes? Why the often exponential level of anxiety and stress, that seems to accompany relationships between the sexes, often leading unabated, onto a road of irrevocable breakups and divorces?

Well, neither have I ......however, as mentioned earlier, I am no clinical psychologist, or anything even remotely close to that profession, but I suspect, I have somehow figured out, some of what I consider to be, the 'root causes' to the apparent mystery and conflict between the sexes, which one would have thought, should not exist, given that such relationships have, by the powers that be, been "ordained" by the Almighty….. and all that………

Again let me qualify, by veiled or direct "disclaimer", my utterings early o'clock, and to reiterate that the lines of this book, do not pretend to provide a solution to the apparent conflicts, but merely seek to raise greater awareness and sensitivities involved in the nuances of the "opposite sex", hence the word <u>opposite here</u> is the operative word….

Back in 2002, someone sent me, what was intended to be bit of humour (as is my usual preferred writing style), where it is claimed, and just to keep it 'light', that quote:

1. Tests have shown that women rate 3% higher in general intelligence than men, although their brain size is smaller, and that most women act "dumb", to make their mates look good.

2. Women are walking radar detectors, - that is why men have difficulty lying to women. Their brains have the ability to integrate and decipher verbal, visual and other signals of body language.

3. Women want lots of sex, with the man she loves while men, just want lots of sex. (Who said that?)

4. When men flirt, they will lower their pitch of voice, while women will raise theirs.

5.   Women talk and think aloud, while men do them silently. As a result, men think women talk too much and are perceived "nags".

6.   Women talk about their problems, as a way of relieving stress. She wants to be heard, not fixed, by being offered advice and solutions.

7.   Speech and words are not a specific brain skill for men, who find it hard to express themselves. That's why they often choose greeting cards with plenty of words inside. (That way, there's less space for them to write….I sure can guess who "invented" that one)…

8.   Women leave men, not because they are unhappy with what he can provide, but because they are emotionally unfulfilled.

9.   Women use an average of 20,000 communication words, sounds, and gestures a day. Men only use about 7,000. (Now you know...)

10. So ergo, if a woman is talking to you, then she likes you. But if she's not talking, you're in trouble!

11. Men are more thick-skinned than women. Literally. Which explains why women have more wrinkles than men? Boys lose their sensitivity to touch, by the time they reach puberty. So where does all that sensitivity go? (All to that one area??)…

12. If a woman is unhappy in her relationship, she can't concentrate on her work. If a man is unhappy at work, he can't focus on his relationship.

13. Men can only do **one thing** at a time. When they stop their car to read a street directory, they also have to turn down the radio. Women's brains are configured for "multi-tasking" performance. They can talk on the phone; watch the TV and cook, all at the same time.

14. Most men get a "brain hemorrhage", after just 20 minutes of clothes shopping. (You're telling me...?)...for women it's more than a therapeutic pastime...it is a "work of art".....

15. When it comes to sex, women need a reason; men just need a place! (Who said that??)

16. 15% to 20% of men have "feminized" brains. About 10% of women have "masculinised" brains; hence the logic, that there are more gays than lesbians in the world.

17. Most women prefer sex with lights off, because they can't bear to see their man enjoying himself (?) Men like lights on – so they can get the woman's name right. (Ouch!)

Yes, what she wants, romantically speaking, is usually the opposite to what he wants (if he had the guts to admit it), but any deviations, would simply have a devastating effect on her 'tender' heart…So keep quiet..

What, the more 'nonchalant' among you might say, so what – that's natures way, it was so since "Adam was a boy", – our parents and grand parents never figured it out, and they went peacefully to the great beyond, accepting the "ce la vie" of it all…

Why do men want to "go", when she wants to "stay"? – Why do men keep "switching" the TV channels with such frequency, as if it were some nervous twitching of the fingers, like some chronic remote recalcitrance, or whatever the 'medics', may wish to call it?

Conversely, what is the cause of 'tele-phone addiction' in females? - What is it that they have to com-municate with such frequency, and in such detail, that the share indices of the likes of AT&T, Sprint, Digicel, Cable and Wireless, or whatever, begin to leap off the charts?

Ever tried watching your wife, girl friend or significant other, on the phone? They actually have to find a comfortable cushion, placed at an acceptable angle, with a foot stool to support their feet, and a glass or cup of whatever, to see them through the 'long haul' that that telephone call is about to become.

Hey, I have observed them myself and to this day, haven't a clue of what subject it is, that requires such minute detail and analysis.

Ask a man "How was you're day?"… His answer… "Fine"… Now ask a woman the same question….and prepare to be "baptized!!"…

As mature adults, we all learn to "live and let live" (if we know what's good for us), – interfere with the ladies in their communications process and you'll soon discover what it is like to be relegated to the "doghouse" for interrupting this 'my life depends on it' call!!

As a strong proponent of a 'balanced life', I note in the "scriptures", we are encouraged to "have faith", to hold on to all the belief, that the future has good things in store for those who set a purpose in life; no matter what age, whether you be 25 running up to 95…no matter…

Pastor Joel Osteen, one of my favourite 'televangelists', was illustrating that point sometime ago, when he referred to a "man in the bible" (no name was given), who was simply described as "the man with the withered hand."

He was asked (by Jesus), to "stretch forth thy hand", and while he had had an ample excuse not to respond, (after all he had a withered hand) , he did in fact attempt to stretch it out, and we are told, he was healed of his ailment.

I say this just to say, don't give up on life, till you become satisfied, that all that you wanted to achieve has been achieved.

You failed that exam, try again, you lost that job – knock on some more doors, your business went bankrupt - find an alternative source of funding it.

Was it Henry Ford, founder of the Ford Motor Company, who went into bankruptcy about 6 or 8 times, trying to get the Ford Motor car on the road in the early 1900's(?)

Then there was Thomas Edison, who tried to get a loan from about three hundred (300) Banks, the first 299 of which, had turned down his applications towards the funding of the first "Light Bulb Project" in the world….gees… – talk about perseverance!!

Had they not proceeded to 'stretch forth thy hand', just think, there would be no Ford Cars and others modeled off the original Ford car (model T?) design, running around the roads of the world today; with lesser mortals like you and I, making payments to the same Banks, to finance them.

Was it not for Mr. Edison's perseverance with his darn incandescent "Light Bulb" Project and the more recent successor inventions (the likes of so called "Energy Savers", or others with Wind and Solar Power), we would literally still "be in the dark?"…

Yes…literally!!...

The opening lines of Chapter Eight of one of my earlier Book Publications titled "My Dog Hamish", released by Athena Press in London, England, in 2003, says, and I quote: "In life, those of us who wish to get ahead, must be prepared, not just to work hard, but to work smart, we must dare to be not just different, but exceptional, we must be prepared to go, where no one else has gone before, setting new standards, new heights, new norms." Unquote.

That my friends is the only formula, for long term success - When you get knocked down, knock yourself up again, When so called friends try to discourage you, use that energy that you would have used to despise them, to drive you further in the pursuance of your goals.

If you take a look around you, you will find, that some of the most successful people, were at one time considered as weird…think the "Einstein types", the "Wright Brothers aircraft project" … crazy or just plain bonkers? I am sure people around would have thought… "Think Bill Gates, the college dropout"… so called 'failures' of their era…but Oh! how they turned their situations around; to the point that, many of us, would give our right arms to have 'failed' like they have…. even right here in the Caribbean, our own Derek Walcott's Literature, prior to the Nobel Prize accolade, would have had his share of rebuffs…. so what???

The secret to their success, is turning that so called "disability", "setback" or "disadvantage", to their great and phenomenal "advantage"… plain and simply – Yes, the "stretch forth thy hand" theory…

Looks like it all makes good sense to me, never mind some would argue, depending on your perspective, its ostensible, controversial 'biblical' origins!!

So what has all this got to do with human gender romance??

On the subject of male and female perspectives, here's another little snippet of humour, that was, again, emailed to me some time ago, by some one from my research " Ambassadors" team overseas; where it advances the rationale, on, "Why Men cannot and Don't Write Advice Columns".

The resulting solution from the following question and answer provided by the 'male columnist' speak for themselves, and went like this:

I quote:

Dear Walter,

I hope you can help me out here.....

The other day, I set off to work leaving my husband in the house watching the TV.... as usual! I hadn't driven more than about five (5) miles down the road, when the engine conked out and the car suddenly shuddered to a halt. I walked back home to get my husband's help; but when I arrived at the house, I couldn't believe my eyes…. He was in our bedroom with my neighbour's daughter.

I'm 32, my husband is 34, and the neighbour's daughter is 22. We have been married for ten years.

When I confronted him, he broke down and admitted that they had been having an affair for the past six months. I told him to stop or I'd leave him. He said he had been let go from his job six months ago and at that point, he had been feeling increasingly depressed and worthless.

I love him very much, but ever since I gave him the ultimatum, he has become increasingly distant. He won't even go to counseling which I had suggested and I'm afraid, I just can't get through to him any more.

Can you please help me with some advice?

Sincerely,

Sheila.

Walter then responds to the desperate lady with the following advice:

Dear Sheila,

A car stalling after being driven such a short distance can be caused by a variety of faults with the engine. Start off by checking that there is no debris in the fuel line.

If it is clear, check the vacuum hard line and hoses on the intake manifold and also check all grounding wires. If none of these approaches solves the problem, it could be that the fuel pump itself is faulty, causing low fuel pressure to the injectors.

I hope this helps you…

Safe driving,

Walter.

Unquote.

OK, this perhaps is an "extreme" illustration of male vs female perspectives, but I believe you catch my drift….the guys haven't a clue most of the time…

CHAPTER THREE (3)

Observation Tower

FROM MY "OBSER-
VATION TOWER"
– namely the
two eyes in the sock-
ets on the front of my
head, and ears equal-
ly attuned to the com-
ments, complaints
and lamentations of
well..."That's how
he is", or... "That's
how she is" attitudes,
I have for sometime,
been 'picking up the vibes' that, when it comes
to relationships between the sexes, men seem
to perceive more of a "series of slots" - much
like the design of a "chest of drawers" into
which compartments, they place the various

components of their life - one drawer for "relationships", one for "religion", one for "family", one for "society", one for "work", one for "play".....you get the drift.....and are somehow able to open and shut those drawers, dependent upon the need or desires of a particular time, keeping the contents of each drawer totally independent from the other, often operating out of each drawer in turn, totally oblivious of the contents of other drawers, almost to the extent that, when one drawer is open, the other drawers are seemingly non existent... Yes, totally oblivious of anything else going on in the world...

This 'compartmentalization' seems to drive women 'berserk' as the female perception of relationships, in contrast, again tends to be totally unlike our "imaginary" chest of drawers.

Instead, it is, at best, more like a "callaloo or pepper pot" a potpurri, a chicken soup, a 'bouyon' – or a large cupboard with no shelves, full of stuff, all mixed up together... call it what you may, but again, you get my drift.... work with me here... a merger of 'all things', where each and everything, touches or mixes with everything else, each impacting on the other...

Yes, she mixes all the "ingredients" of her life, into this "internet type soup" with the flavor of each ingredient, impacting on the flavour of the other, to the extent, that if any of the ingredients become 'contaminated' by whatever other stimulus, especially those of the 'relationships' variety, very soon, the whole 'pot' metamorphoses into an awful taste, often to the extent, that the whole darn bowl of soup, gets thrown out!

This seems to explain, why, in my humble view, our women see life from an 'Instead Of' Perspective (or window), while their men seem to view the same situation from an 'In addition to' perspective.

Men buy new clothes (occasionally), yet hold on to the old ones for years, even though they clearly "will never fit me again" sort of situation; while women would, on the other hand, buy new dresses (frequently), and are very generous to the garage sales, to help make space for incoming (unexpected), merchandise.

Interestingly enough though, included in the strategy in finding a garage sale or pawn shop, is finding one that is as far away from the home base as possible, as there is no way "that other woman"(whoever she may be), should be seen wearing "my dress".

I think I am picking up something to that effect, which, from my 'little' observation tower, I still have not been sufficiently able to decipher.

So let us "shift gears" for just a moment....Ah! The beauty of "spontaneous writing"...

In the world of Business, Industry and Commerce and indeed within the ranks of the Private Sector, Public Sector and their related "parastatal" affiliations, numerous man hours (or is that person hours?), of productive time, is lost through workers, (and indeed employers, as individuals), having to 'nurse' the often unspoken trauma, that accompanies a 'mismatch' at the domestic level with their significant other, especially in what is purported to be, our life long relationships; and the implied or legal 'permanence" of a marriage.

Like a 'Cancer to Productivity' the inner rumblings pervade everything they do, everywhere they go, sometimes to the extent, that the situation results in health issues, enormous stress, insanity, even domestic violence, suicides, and other forms of trauma; sometimes even premature "earthly demise"....just seems like their world has caved in....

Just think how much more productive we could be if our 'romantic traumas' did not encroach into our career life, or better still, managed more effectively.

No matter how we try to 'mask' it, that all pervading cancer is ever present, like an 'all consuming fire' of incompatibility... Trust me... I've been there...and later, without having the answers myself, tried to 'assist' many others, alluding to similar situations - in my travels worldwide...

The solution to my mind seems to rest in finding some form of methodology, that would, at least, minimize, or help us mitigate (I did not say eliminate, as I suspect that would be wishful thinking), chances for an 'oil and water mix' which, as we all know, is no mix at all.

We need to find a way to "bridge the gap" of the often mental incompatibility, that seems to infiltrate the intended "harmony" which, according to the master plan, should be inherent in our adult liaisons and interactions...yet the mystery between these two beautiful beings continues unabated.... count yourself 'lucky' when you find a moment of "Utopia"...try to understand what you did 'right' and do that again...

But I would caution that the "methodology" which seemed "right" on Monday, might very well deteriorate during the week, and so, by Friday afternoon, - you've got it "wrong" again... keep on trying my friend....

"MARRY HER AND YOU'LL SEE"

Back in the days of my (second) bachelorhood, when I used to 'come and go' as I wished, I recall visiting a Beach Resort one day, bright and sunny, in the middle of a typical Caribbean weekend, when I ran into a group of "senior" gentlemen, strategically positioned at the far end of the Resorts swimming pool.

As I passed by, they called out to me, to come and join them... they had been persuing a bit of what I alluded to earlier, as 'window shopping' around the pool, admiring the better 'feline forms' as they darted to and fro, in the latest designer bikini swim wear...an "eye candy" session... sort of thing...you ladies have no idea of the "things" you do to us, just be "showing up"...

Anyway, for them (my group of senior gentlemen... and I am talking professionals here), it was like a free fashion show, and they were all quite visibly excited about it, as they sipped on their favourite "libations"…

Being the bachelor that I was back then, I assured them, that while I agreed that selected 'feline forms' were certainly deserving as being classified as 'eye candy', the scenario they were witnessing, was, at that time, not a novelty to me.

After all, as bachelor 'Numero Uno' I had been out on Party Cruises, Beach Parties, House Parties, Pyjama Parties, you name it, that the sighting of an army of 'beauties' had practically, (if I can say so myself), become 'routine'; so I declined the invitation to sit by, and join what I then regarded as simply 'senior citizens' fun.

This (my decline), did not seem to go down too well with the small group of gentlemen, especially when I alluded to having 'seen it all before'…Oh the arrogance of it all…one might say….

"Do you have a girlfriend?" – was the next question…

"Yes I do" was my reply, and "Does she allow you to admire 'the beauties' while she is with you?"

"Yes she does, and even points out certain models, whom she thinks I might like to scan" …was my come back.

"Well we don't have such a privilege when we are out with our wives you know" – "Somehow they seem to resent us doing any 'ogling' of other female forms, especially when they are around, and that's why we are here, doing it on our own… It helps feel like 'young men' again.."

"Well, my lady is different, we always have a 'laugh' over such matters" I responded…"need to take a break from it sometimes…"

"Oh yes, well enjoy it while it lasts" was the come back.

"What do you mean? – Is she (my lady) going to 'change'?" was my naïve, perhaps even 'sarcastic', response…

"Well, what you have sounds nice, but from our experience, she could very well be a 'slick' one you know"… they added.

Getting perhaps a bit defensive, I came back with "Well I don't consider, and I don't believe, that my lady is anything of a 'con' artist!!!"

"Well my friend" they said, "Have it your way… Have it your way."

As I stood there in a, perhaps, hesitating defence mode, thinking to myself – 'Why the heck are these old guys putting my lady down – they don't even know her'…

With my own intrigue seemingly apparent to them, they drove home their final point …

"Don't worry about us young fellow, just marry her and you'll see - We were all like you at one time you know…Don't worry with us!" At that point, I recall feeling a sense of 'disdain' for the Group, most of whom at the time, were several times my senior.

A number of them have since died, while others are now considered among the 'elderly'…poor 'guys'.

But you know something, years later, and now that I too have arrived at my more 'senior' years, married with domestic constraints, responsibilities and obligations; I would have to concede, that those 'senior' gentlemen of the day, were right… coming and going as you wish, sure had its 'plusses', being able to 'create' formula for the 'sustainability' of your masculinity sure had its place; the age old "eye-candy" thing….. but then, the laws of nature have it, that we must ultimately hang up our boots and grow up, as we will inevitably face a different 'drum beat' whether willingly, or unwillingly, after we marry….count on it….

I am not prepared at this point, to even attempt go into any details of what you might expect, as no doubt, this will vary from situation to situation, but what I do know, is that a certain 'metamorphosis', does occur in the female brain, once her man says "I do"…lets leave it at that…

This is apparently what the 'old guys' meant, when they said, "Marry her and you will see".

So my young "Adonis" prepare to make mental, physical and emotional adjustments, as you walk back down that aisle – remember the "aisle, altar, hymn" theory.

My Dad used to say, there was "no great hurry" to rush into marriage before you are ready you know…..it is not a "pot of gold" or "bed of roses", so take it to 'bursting point' before you say "I do!"

He was in his late 30's, (in fact almost 40 years old), when he first married my Mom and I arrived, (as his first born), about five years later; but as many did back then, they made it first time round, to the proverbial "till death do us part", and this they did, in what they had described to me, and my siblings, as a lifelong 'perpetual courtship'.

So what do they know??

Well my friends, just listen up to the 'senior folks' – there is no substitute for their experience, they knew what they were saying, yes they know what they are talking about – believe me...... they have been tried and tested and came out 'trumps'... no matter your "know it all" youthful opinion..... "Bless them".

CULTURAL LITERACY

On a different yet related note, a phe-nomenon which, in my childhood, dur-ing the colonial era, did not form part of the lexicon of my up-bringing, and which, through a greater un-derstanding of the lit-eracy works of no less a personage than St.  Lucian born Nobel Laureate, Derek Walcott, I have now since, come to a greater degree of comprehen-sion of our own "environmental" origins...

I speak here of what is referred to as 'Cultural Literacy' and from what I now seem to understand, it is the "apparent knowledge and ability, to read the landscape of your own life, your environment and the people within it", and all of the nuances that relate to its success.

It places emphasis on the facts and knowledge of your environment, (in such a manner), which persons who are foreign, or unfamiliar with it, are clearly unable to read.

To be 'Culturally Literate' therefore, as opposed to 'Literate' by the measure of a 'dominant culture', (as the one time colonial powers purported to be), is to possess the basic information, as may be required, to thrive within your own environment, even in the so called modern day world in which we live.

As I ponder on this phenomenon, I recall in the early days of my career, working as a then 'Trainee Manager', in what was also then referred to as the 'Green Gold Era', when banana production, and exports, were regarded as the 'salvation' of the economy of my home town.

I used to visit the plantations on "agronomic" field visits, to witness the production and harvesting of the fruit, first hand, in the field; under the tutelage of my then expatriate 'bosses' whose demeanor often spoke volumes as to their perception, that, farmers, and farm workers, were largely illiterate persons, not having acquired the basic reading, writing and arithmetic skills, that were upheld as central to any form of upward mobility…

In contrast to that notion, I was never-the-less often fascinated by these same farmers; in their ability to read the weather, read planting and harvesting cycles, read and understand the harvesting and packaging techniques, (as had been 'imposed' by the International High Street supermarket chains, thousands of miles across the Atlantic), and who even had the ability, to 'beat the system', by ensuring that they got maximum returns, for even their under grade fruit!!

I recall one particular farmer, on the island of St. Vincent, being able to tell what time of the day it was with 'military accuracy', – a man who had never owned a watch or clock in his life and, even if he did, could not read the time; while those of us who were supposed to have excelled in the '3R's ('reading, riting, rithmetic') could never dream to match what he, as if by natural instincts, was unquestionably able to do.

A quick glance by this perceived "illiterate" farmer at the sky, or even a shadow cast by the sun, produced an accurate assessment of the time of day, to which the manufacturers of Seiko, Cartier and Rolex amongst others, could only begin imagine....their 'educated' CEO's could soon be out of work, with 'illiterates' so adept at time keeping as that of our "St.Vincent" farmer...

The question then is, "Who exactly is literate" (as opposed to illiterate), and who is it that determines the measure of the two ostensible opposites?? – Who??…

Yes, while we understand the need to conform to International standards, as set by the so called 'first world', in order to 'get by' within that world, the alternative world, where "Cultural Literacy" as I believe I have understood it thus, must not be frowned upon or even 'overtly' denigrated; as it is evident, that if persons who are perceived as 'Literate' by first world standards, were relocated to an environment, (such as the farmer alluded to earlier), they would find themselves totally lost, 'malfunction and non productive' in the 'Culturally Literate' environment….so "to thine own self be true".

Now let us try to return to the theme of this book; as I have said all of the above just to say, that the same 'concept' applies to your relationships and the environment in which they operate.

To become 'Culturally Literate' to the norms of your own home and domestic situation, in other words, to be able to "analyse", and respond, to your own situation, is to begin to chart the course of success; for yourself and, indeed, for your family within it.

Moving along…..

CHAPTER FOUR (4)

Retail Therapy

NOW TO CHANGE THE subject and tone just a bit… if I may!

You may be 'surprised' to know, that during my Research on the preparation of this book, that a number of ladies (of both regional and international origin), told me of the 'high', the 'buzz', they get, from shopping – aka… 'Retail Therapy' in other words.

In fact, one retired 'senior' lady admitted, that she would go down to the Mall to have a look around and buy stuff, and when she got back home, would all but wonder, why on earth she had bought the articles.

So a week or so later, she would take the articles back to the shop, (complete with original packaging), only to end up buying some more "stuff" she again did not want!

What exactly is this quest among our ladies of all ages??...Is this something to do with the 'hunt' in all of us, and indeed, the bane of the male gender, when it comes to 'chasing down' the opposite sex? ...

Can it be classified as a, 'just for fun', sort of thing??

I am still trying to find answers to unlocking the secrets of some of these mysterious behaviors in human gender...

In the world of computers, there is something called a 'password'... yes, common knowledge you say... agreed... that notwithstanding, it gives us the key to gaining access, via your 'PC/Laptop', or whatever, onto the global network or 'Information Highway'.

You have got to learn and memorise that 'password' as, without it, you cannot access the system; no matter how important you believe yourself to be in the overall 'technological' equation.

All of you ICT wizards out there, I am sure, could give me a lesson or two on the subject...

Well my friends have you ever asked yourself, "What is the 'password' to your woman's heart?"

Indeed, what is the 'password' to your heart? - She also needs to have it...

Do you know what it is... even for your own self??

As alluded to earlier, there is now this global phenomenon, referred to as "Retail Therapy" which, in a word, simply means 'going shopping'.

Women have turned that process into an art form, and spend hours researching the desired product, putting energy into it, that men can only marvel at!

But before we delve deeper, into the nuances of Retail Therapy, perhaps I could quote, from the content of an article I came across, in my home town Voice Newspaper (penned by E. Victor M.), which sought to posit, that: "Men are just happier people" in this world, due if only, to the simplicity of our expectations, where he says, and I quote:

"Happier? Well, perhaps just in some ways, as this short piece attempts to explore select areas in which our (male) situation in life, makes things a little easier for us, than for our better halves; the fairer sex, the ones who have been dubbed, 'deadlier than the male!!'

They say men can never understand women... but to women, we (men), are an open book, especially where there are twists and turns in the way of looking at things; we are considered to deal with situations logically and simply; so we may be seem happier then, just because, compared to them, we are relatively simple.

And just what is it that you expect from such simple creatures?

Well, in marriage, your last name stays put. The garage is all yours. Wedding plans usually take care of themselves. Chocolate is just another snack. You can never be pregnant. You can wear a white T-shirt to a water park; in fact, you can wear NO shirt to a water park. Car mechanics tend to tell you the truth.

Caribbean guys especially listen up to this next one...The world is your urinal; .... (So where do you expect us to dispose of all that Piton Beer?)... When overseas especially, you never have to drive to another gas station restroom, because this one is just too "icky." You don't have to stop and think of which way to turn a nut on a bolt. Same work, more pay! Wrinkles add character; Wedding dress=$5000, Tux rental=$100. People never stare at your chest when you're taking to them; the occasional well rendered 'burp' is practically expected; new shoes don't cut, blister or mangle your feet; one mood all the time 24/7; phone conversations are over in 30 seconds flat; 'you know stuff about tanks.'

Then, a five-day vacation requires only one suitcase. You can open all your own jars. You get extra credit for the slightest act of thoughtfulness. If someone forgets to invite you, he, or she, can still be your friend. Your underwear is $8.95 for a three-pack. Three pairs of shoes are more than enough. You almost never have 'strap' problems in public. You are unable to see wrinkles in your clothes.

Even more, everything on your face stays its original colour (never mind the grey beard). The same hairstyle lasts for years, maybe even decades. You only have to shave your face and neck. You can play with toys all your life. Your belly usually hides your big hips. One wallet and one pair of shoes... one colour for all seasons. You can wear shorts no matter how your legs look. You can 'do' your nails with a pocket knife. You have freedom of choice concerning growing a mustache. You can do Christmas shopping for 25 relatives on December 24 in just 25 minutes!!....

So, 'no wonder men are happier'"... Unquote.

Well is it that, as we grow up, in our homes, and the wider society; that little girls are 'conditioned' differently to little boys, or, is the distinction simply 'inherent' to the male/female 'DNA'?

I am not sure... but, what I do know, is that somehow, ladies are able to derive great pleasure from going shopping, as compared to their partners; of the opposite gender.

I recall sitting with a 'bunch of guys' in the cocktail lounge, downstairs at 'Macys' megastore in downtown New York, some time ago; while wives, girlfriends or significant others, were upstairs 'shopping' their hearts out.

The Macys Board of Directors was clearly most perceptive, to have recognised that in order to maximize their Store sales, they had to find a way to 'park' the men somewhere, in a manner that this would not interrupt the 'scientific process' being conducted by the ladies, being in their 'research mode' on the upper floors.

All it took, to keep the men 'in one place', was a cocktail lounge, or Sports Bar, with pleasantly attired lady bartenders, and an overhead large screen television, (tuned to the latest Sports Channel telecast).

Boy, the men did not want to move, even after their wives had completed their research and descended upon their lounge, laden with bags and baskets, seeking desperately to get 'their men' to escort them to the car, or bus, or whatever vehicle it was, that got them to the store in the first place.

No, I don't have the answer, but I will quickly admit, that I certainly enjoyed being down in that Macys Lounge hanging out with the guys myself... hey!... some of us have become 'friend for life' and added to my email list...

I recall that some of the guys there, even had the inspired thought, that their ladies might as well make some further rounds at other stores in the area, and meet them "back at Macys Lounge" after they had completed their extended research... so delightful was the setting... a bar, a TV with the latest sports channel, pleasantly attired cocktail wait-resses...going where you say??

So there you are....

In lighter vein, one my of lady 'researchers' (you'd better start getting used to this writing style), again sent me a bit of humour, which, she says, was written by a Lady for the Ladies titled: "It's good to be a man".

Again it goes something like this, and which, I believe, follows closely as a form of amplified version of the previous "Men are Happier" theory:

1. Your 'ass' is never a factor in a job interview. 2. Your orgasms are real - Yes always. 3. Your last name stays put. 4. The garage is all yours. 5. Wedding plans take care of themselves. (We had these before) 6. You never feel compelled to stop a friend from getting laid. 7. Car mechanics tell you the truth. 8. You don't give a 'rat's ass' if someone notices your new haircut. 9. Hot wax never comes near our pubic area. 10. Same work more pay. 11. Wrinkles add character. 12. You don't have to leave the room to make emergency crotch adjustments. 13. Wedding Dress $5000.00; Tux rental $100. 14. If you retain water, it's in a canteen. 15. People never glance at your chest when you're talking to them. 16. New shoes don't cut, blister, or mangle your feet. 7. Porno movies are designed with you in mind. 18. Your pals can be trusted never to ask you, "So, you notice anything different?" 19. One mood, ALL the damn time. 20. Phone conversations are over in 30 seconds. 21. A five-day vacation requires only one suitcase. 22. You can open all your own jars. 23. Dry cleaners and hair cutters don't rob you blind. 24. You can go to a public toilet, without a

support group. 25. You can leave the motel bed un-made. 26. You get extra credit for the slightest act of thoughtfulness. 27. If someone forgets to invite you to something, you can still be friends. 28. Your underwear is now $10 for a three-pack. 29. If you are 34 and single, nobody notices. 30. Everything on your face stays its original colour. 31. You can quietly enjoy a car ride from the passenger's seat. 32. Three pairs of shoes are more than enough.

Next up...# 33... You don't have to clean your apartment if the meter reader is coming. 34. You can quietly watch a game with your buddy for hours without ever thinking "he must be mad at me." 35. No maxi-pads. 36. You don't munch off others deserts. 37. You can drop by to see a friend without having to bring a little gift. 38. If another guy shows up at the party in the same outfit, you just might become lifelong friends. 39. You are not expected to know the names of more than five colours. 40. You don't have to stop and think which way to turn a nut on a bolt. 41. You almost never have strap problems in public. 42. You are unable to see wrinkles in your clothes. 43. The same hair-style lasts for years, maybe decades. 44. You don't have to shave below your neck. 45. Your belly usu-ally hides your big hips. 46. One wallet and one pair of shoes, one colour, all season. 47. You can 'do' your nails with pocket knife. 48. You have free-dom of choice, concerning growing a moustache. 49. Christmas shopping can be accomplished for 25 relatives on December 24th, in 45 minutes. And finally # 50…. The world is your urinal!!!

Well I suppose a bit of 'humorous repetition' doesn't hurt, if only it serves to highlight the often unspoken differences, in the perspectives of the two genders, and help reduce the looming 'tensions' that often accompany not knowing anything at all of your life companions inherent and unspoken view point.

Moving along…

CHAPTER FIVE (5) -

Flicks and Soaps

WHAT IS IT WITH the (chick) "Flicks and Soaps" that clears the office of its female human resources - or at least used to in my early days as an office junior; creating a mass exodus with an instant vacant space, at a set time of the day (just about closing time especially), anywhere an operating television set may have been absent?

Yes, in one of my earlier jobs in an Admin and Accounting office, I recall 'the ladies of the office' exiting the building with military precision, at a set time each day, to go watch 'the soaps' on TV.

I even decided to try it out myself one day, to see if I could find out what all the excitement was about, and subsequently came to the conclusion, even back then, that the 'Hollywood psychologists' had mastered the art of playing to the natural instincts and emotions of the 'average' female down to a fine art, and in their own right, escalating the ratings of whatever TV channel they represented, to an exponential level.

The sad part of it all, to my mind, was that those (younger) ladies of the day, even began to believe, that the romantic intrigues of the 'soap operas' could become a 'bench mark' for their own lives, and decision making processes.

Wrong, you have just been set up my girl... go listen to what your Mom or Grandma have to say – she has way more answers to life's problems than the "Hollywood" writers; that is not how real life was intended to be, never mind the 'grandiose window dressing' that is portrayed as being the way life ought to be...

Trust me; those so called 'rich and famous' movie stars have some of the most 'screwed up' lives you could ever imagine!!...

Don't get caught up in a fantasy you may never be able to effectively manage, causing your own home and family to fall apart....

The following lines of humour, yet again, may be a case in point....

(a) BEFORE MARRIAGE....

He: 'Yes. At last. It was so hard to wait.'

She: 'Do you want me to leave?'

He: 'No! Don't even think about it.'

She: 'Do you love me?'

He: 'Of course! Over and over!'

She: 'Have you ever cheated on me?'

He: 'No! Why are you even asking?'

She: 'Will you kiss me?'

He: 'Every chance I get.'

She: 'Will you hit me?'

He: 'Are you crazy? I'm not that kind of person!'

She: 'Can I trust you?'

He: 'Yes'

She: 'Darling!'

(b) AFTER MARRIAGE….

You just simply read from bottom to top - taken with a "pinch of salt!"

So be careful what those 'soaps' are doing to your mind, and indeed, the minds of your young sons or daughters, who may also be watching along with you…

One day, they will be all grown up and in need of a 'sustainable benchmark' for themselves, as they seek to champion the best interests of their own families.

Your responsibility is to ensure, that as far as is practical, they be given the 'right' exposure…an exposure which would, in the inevitable tough times, help them navigate the stormy waters of their own lives….

I commend my own parents, for the part they played, in shaping my own thought processes, even though I may not have 'liked' the apparent 'strict' methods they applied to me, and to perhaps a lesser extent, my siblings.

SEX APPEAL AND SELECTION CRITERIA

Over the years of my 'research', I had been attempting to find out, just what are the 'pull factors' that determine which 'criteria' are used, (by both men and women), in their 'first sight' selection of a potential lifetime 'partner' process.

You know what I mean... the 'window shopping' that both genders, without speaking, conduct when out and about, that could, over time, decide the generational direction of their family tree?

The reasons gathered were not as diverse as one would imagine, given the numerous permutations of 'gender design', but the logic in the female criteria in particular, continues to elude me even more, but first, I'll start with my findings on " the men".

A man in a 'window shopping mode' might wish to describe himself, based on his personal likes and dislikes, as, say, a 'pretty face' man (boy... I just love a pretty face), or a 'boobs' man, a 'hairstyle type' man, a 'derriere'(bottoms) man, a 'Coca Cola bottle' packaging man'(don't we all guys ?)... even an 'ankle man'; all in one way or another, suggesting what I would describe as "the wow factor"... the 'factor' that causes HIM to get up off his 'perch' and go over to her, with some version of the line, "Hi I'm Andrew, and I was wondering whether I could buy you a drink (or lunch or even a car, or a house, or an island)"… you get my drift?

I rather suspect that 'most things' are a turn on for us guys; never mind our so called varying "degrees of sophistication…"

The point here, is to identify exactly what motivated the 'first move' by him (quite apart from the underlying testosterone motives), that could ultimately launch into orbit - a friendship, or relationship, a marriage, a family…whatever.

In fact, while I am at it, let me explore a bit deeper, the 'ankle man' situation with the following "revealing" little story…

Some years ago, I was at the Airport with a one time business colleague, awaiting the arrival of a 'V.I.P. delegation' for a Conference our Company was meant to be hosting on the island.

As we sat in the Airport waiting lounge, I looked across and saw my colleague, with eyes fixated on a particular lady standing in a queue…

No big deal, that's what guys do, we just can't help it, and quite often don't even realize it when we are staring.

So anyway, what came next was his 'profound' and again mysterious statement, inviting me to "look at that lady over there" – she's "really strong, sexy, a vision of beauty" perhaps beyond all others at the Airport terminal at the time, (man, this stuff can happen to you anywhere)…

I looked across at his 'stunning vision of beauty' and thought to myself, well yes, I see the lady you are drawing my attention to, but not being exactly in mental 'sync' with his level of enthusiasm, I asked "What is it about her that you find so magnetic?" – "Her Ankles, man…he said, her ankles!!"

Not having heard that one before, nor ever even thought of it, I responded, "Her ankles? What is it about her ankles?"

His response was "Her ankles, they are screaming out that she is a strong and exciting woman" – I then began a 'study' of the 'ankles'; exhibit myself thinking now just how do you connect ankles with (sexy) excitement? "Hey, I'm not here to put down your 'turn on', your judgment or whatever, but to be honest, I am not sure I share or even understand your enthusiasm on the subject… just what are you on about man??"

"Don't you see her ankles man? Don't you see?"

"Yes I see the ankles my friend, but they don't seem to be doing anything for me... 'no comprende' – but if it is your thing, well then go for it..."

Much to be said for a conversation between two Business Executives awaiting the arrival of a flight at an Airport terminal (of all places), but to this day, I have not been able to decipher, the nexius between the ankles "exhibit" and the seemingly overwhelming excitement my business colleague was expressing.

Maybe someone will help me figure it out someday, but that logic continues too elude me to this day on my journey of research into the 'pull factors' which influence and help prompt the genesis of all (at least in the Western model), adult Human relationships.

With that off my chest, let me head back to where I left off earlier, and to share the results of my research among 'the women' samples of which emanate geographically anywhere from the British Midlands to Europe - to South Florida, the Far East and right here in the Caribbean...

The 'generic' female look out for "tall, dark and handsome men" is still, I believe, as legend has it, the (oft unspoken), centre plank of the selection criteria, as might be deliberated upon by most up and coming professional women, as their "radars" scan the landscape for potential partners.

Having said that, I note, in more recent times, and in select situations, a shift in the selection criteria, to the 'toy boy' partnerships, where a slightly 'older' female teams up domestically with a 'younger' male; often several times her junior...the female "cougar" era seems to have arrived....

In fact, I was reading an article by one Dr Judith Sills, not so long ago in a Lifestyle internet publication titled "Six Reasons you'll find love After 40".

In her article, she posits that "you might be skeptical about the possibilities of a meaningful (late), entry into real life - which you may consider 'limits the possibilities'; but the fact is that, 'single, divorced or widowed' women can 'create' meaningful, loving relationships at 40,50,60... and so on and on."

She continues, that while men "rarely lose their attraction to young flesh and often look right past ripe "fruit", other things (possibilities), are also true that help make "loving connections" likely to appear in later life.

Among the six considerations for the 'late bloomer' are, she says:

1. This time, you don't need a "provider".
2. This time, you don't need to please your parents.
3. This time, you can't get pregnant.
4. Older men, open hearts.
5. More time, more money means more romance.
6. What's meaningful means something different now!...

If you want more of this I suggest you look up Dr Sills on Lifestyle, whom, I gather, is a trained clinical psychologist, and author of some five best-sellers....

Now back to my earlier mention of the "female" selection criteria and the often 'ball park' statement, of the "tall, dark and handsome" profile, which, I considered, needed some delving into a bit deeper, in order to find out, what exactly are our gorgeous ladies looking for as the initial 'pull factor'.....just what is it that makes their faces light up as you the guys go by - never mind their often awkward attempts at 'masking' their expressions?

The results of my research again left me with more questions than answers, with responses as varied as the range of ladies making up the research samples, and whom I managed to 'interview' at my various geographical locations.

But if you thought that the guy with the 'ankles fetish' seemed a bit strange, wait till you hear this for a 'common denominator' in the survey for an initial "pull factor" by the ladies…. wait for it guys – its your **SHOES**!!…

Yep!… the logic continues to fly straight past me every time, but that's what the fair ladies from the samples "interviewed" seem to be saying about the "entry level" criteria, of the potential 'father of their kids'.

Well of course, once you start probing a bit deeper, you will begin to hear more of the real 'long term' (in depth), and 'nesting' criteria coming through like 'a good education', a good job, kind and thoughtful, a nice car, house, from a good family, likes children, goes to church, the size of his 'package' (put your own interpretation to that one guys); but the point of my exercise, was to find out what is it that creates the initial 'pull factor'; to be of sufficient magnetism, that would lead you to even bother to get up and find out at all, about all the other 'long term' criteria, as I have alluded to above.

Listen up now gentlemen, don't go breaking down the doors of your local shoe stores on the premise of this 'mysterious gem' of information.

In fact, I must quickly put in my own 'disclaimer' clause, similar to that which you find on the labels of a new food product, indicating to the effect that "These statements have not been evaluated by the 'XYZ' Administration. This product is not intended to diagnose, treat, cure or prevent any disease".... you know what I mean.... pinch of salt guys, pinch of salt!!

Anyway, like yourself, I too am mystified, but would disclose that much of my research was conducted in Restaurants, Bars, Pubs, Clubs and other places; perhaps where 'anything you say cannot be held against you', as opposed to Offices, Board Rooms, College Classes, Libraries, Churches and other places, associated with greater depth of thought.

SEX APPEAL AND THE SENSES

Another component of the sexual allure, commonly known as 'Sex Appeal' as I understand it, is the sound of your voice.

The tone or 'pitch' of the 'voice' is said to unconsciously signal the potential degree of your masculinity or femininity.

High pitched voices tend to be associated with higher estrogen hormone levels in females; while lower pitched voices tend to signal higher levels of the male hormone known as testosterone.

Hence the "illusion" that to have a "sexy" voice is to speak in either a high pitched voice (as in nubile women), or that deep (Teddy Pendergrass) voice - or whatever other deep tone, that is associated with ostensible male virility.

In fact, Mother Nature is said to have programmed women in such a manner, as to even exhibit 'variable' voice tones; these fluctuate with the degree of the onset or egress of ovulation.

Clearly, our so called 'ferro - magnetism' is triggered by a number of, if not all of, our senses, of sight, sound, taste and smell.

Have heard it said that the act of kissing provides the 'taste' while 'pheromones' provide the smell, latter to which, I can personally attest.

Hey, don't under estimate the 'smell factor' as I for one, had earlier, mentally relegated it to going back to the 'cave man' days; until one day, I recall sitting at my office desk at work back in the early 80's, in as totally an unromantic setting as you can get if you ask me, when a young lady, one of my then staff members to be exact, came up alongside me, to discuss an exercise she had been working on.

As I looked over the documentation - of course fully regaled with my 'professional hat' firmly fixed upon my head - I was suddenly 'hit for six' by a certain aroma emanating from the young lady next to me, which blew my concentration right out of the water.

This resulted in my having to 'fight like mad' to stave off the temptation to switch my attention to her, rather than on what she had brought in to discuss with me.

After all, I was at work, and even the "head of the department" at that time, and there was no way I was going to allow myself to be accused of what today is likely to be referred to as "sexual harassment at the work place..." no way...

But boy, did I have to put up a heck of a 'fight' on my own emotional instincts, trying (and hopefully succeeding), to conceal the rumblings of the 'turbo driven internal combustion engine' that was going on inside me, and therefore my only choice, as it seemed, was to stay clear of any "close encounters" with this lady at the work place, or pursue those instincts to my own detriment; but I will be quite honest and admit, that that of itself, was no easy task.

I was determined to maintain the fight over the forces of nature and chose to "stay clear"; but man (as we say in the Caribbean); I have never forgotten the "close encounter"..... That was a close shave which, I suspect, the young lady was not even fully aware of... she probably even thought of me as some kind of 'stuffy boss' or whatever....

All of that notwithstanding, can someone help us out here, with a simple explanation on the sex appeal process, so that there is something plausible to report, to say to the next generation, 'How I met your mother' or 'How I chose your father?'

While in the words of one famous televangelist: 'Love at first sight is often cured with a second look!!'... You may just not be that lucky!

Be careful therefore, with what the 'pull factor' may be, whether it be the 'BMI' (Body Mass Index), or whatever 'first sight' that *'grabs ya' maybe, as it can determine the future genetic direction, of the next generation of your family in whatever form it may take, literally, "for better or for worse".*

CHAPTER SIX (6)

Ooops.....There it is...

FOLLOWING ALONG FROM THE theme of my previous paragraph, in my college student days back in the UK Midlands, I recall meeting a young lady (yes, yet another one), who was herself a (part time), Business

Studies Student, and who had a 'fiancé' who worked as an Accountant with one of the local Accounting Firms.

A group of us got talking socially one evening (at the pub), and started discussing the 'pros and cons' of identifying a compatible life partner, and this particular young lady seemed to feel quite confident that she had "found the answer".

Knowing from my experience up till then, that life does not offer up any "real guarantees", I decided to probe her mind for more information, which at first, she was reluctant to disclose.........

Presumably recognising my own reservations on her having "found the answer", she later said, 'she would invite me to her home one weekend for drinks and dinner so I could meet her partner.'

The date and time having been set, I showed up at her address and was welcomed with: "This is Harry and these are his two kids – aged seven and nine" (if I recall them correctly).

They were kids from his previous marriage, of whom he had taken custody.

On being ushered to a seat in the living area and "niceties" over, we began to converse about the 'mystery' of life, and the 'hit and miss' syndrome which seemed to pervade the world of adult dating and partner identification, of which my College friend had already apprised her partner of my interest, and as a subject of a previous conversation she had with me.

"Malcolm and I" she says to Harry, "were talking after classes sometime ago, about whether it was at all possible, to find a life partner, with whom you could feel comfortably compatible, and without all the usual 'hits and misses'- Shall we tell him our secret?"

All that time, I observed that my two friends, were displaying signs of natural affection, which at one point, I even began to suspect, might have been put on (staged), "for my benefit!"

No, that was not the case - the two were clearly a "house on fire", each madly in love with the other.

"So what's the secret formula?" I asked once again. "Just how and when did you two meet?"

"It was a computer job" Harry said…. "Did you guys work on computers together at one time?"– was my come back…

"No, we met through one of the Computer Dating Agencies here in the UK."

"Just how does that sort of thing work?" I pursued. "Well" Harry proffered, "you go in and register with one of the more reputable, lets call it 'dating agencies' – they are sort of set up for 'busy' persons, who feel they are ready to settle down, but don't have the time (or appetite), for the numerous dates you have to go through before you can find anything close to being your "soul mate."

"They have a sort of questionnaire, which you are asked to fill out, covering some two hundred aspects of your life, under various sub headings such as – Educational, Professional, Sporting, Social, Religious, Ethnic, Partner Preferences, Food Preferences, Cultural, Languages and the list goes on."

"Once you have filled out this list and done the financial registration bit, the Agency goes through a preliminary matching process, out of data already held in their database, and ultimately produce two or three names of potential 'compatibles.'"

"A lunch date is then set up, with one of these 'shortlisted' persons, and if upon meeting, you find 'chemistry' then you are free to 'keep on dating' till you both decide."

"On the other hand, if your "spirits clash" first time round, you have the option of going back to the Agency for a 'rendezvous' with another person from the shortlist, and this goes on, until you both indicate that the proverbial 'chemistry' has kicked in."

Back then, as it was in the late 70's, I was personally amazed, to learn of such a process, and while this 'scientific' approach tended to blow the notion of romantic liaisons right out of the water, it became apparent, that there was merit to the approach, especially if the 'chemistry' exhibited, between my new found friends, was any measure.

I did get the forms, as I too was, at the time, 'weighing options' for the future, but rather than Register, I decided to design my personal list of characteristics by which I might assess my own compatibility, with any future encounters, that came my way.

You know, the formula works, albeit as a less structured model, as it stands to reason, that logically, if you don't know who you are or what you're looking for, how the 'devil' are you going to recognise it when it comes your way!

I came up with my own "ten (10) point" compatibility formula, and discovered, that your "sole mate" may, very well, be right under your nose, but you didn't recognise her (or him), as you searched the globe for that so called "special" person.

Of course, nature being as it is, there is no guarantee, that over time, your significant other, won't start trying to change you into something she or he has designed in the theatre of their minds, rather than accept you as the ideal partners, you thought yourselves to be, when you first met.

This reminds me yet again, of a bit of "internet humour" I came across sometime ago, which went like this...

"Through the ages, men have been trying to unlock the mystery whereby, why do their wives, who accepted them just the way they were before they got married; begin the endless journey to change their behavior and life-style, once their vows are exchanged."

Finally, the 'riddle' is solved, by a somewhat amusing social-scientist, who arrived at this seemingly simple and logical explanation.

"When the bride, accompanied by her father, starts to walk slowly down the aisle, she sees the altar at the end, and hears the choir singing the hymn.

Walking down the aisle, there is a conditioning process, where the brain absorbs these three stimuli: "aisle, altar, and hymn" begins. She becomes mesmerized, as she continually reinforces these perceptions: aisle, altar, and hymn, until finally, as she stops beside the groom, the conditioning process is complete.

She looks up at him, smiling sweetly, and keeps saying to herself… "I'll alter him!"

So for the rest of his life she pursues her "vow" to make him the man she thinks he ought to be….yes "I'll alter him"… guys, just don't resist the fight…

Ooops…there it is…..

On a more serious note, I am inclined to consider (and again, this is just my opinion), that the fundamental difference between men and women, when it comes to marriage planning, is that women tend to plan quite intensely for their "wedding", while men, well,… tend to be more preoccupied with plans for the 'marriage'.

What's the difference you say?

Lots of differences….

The 'Wedding' is a symbolic event, where the new 'stars of the day' shine at their brightest – The Diamonds, The Church, The Music, The Yards of Fabric, The Band, The Reception, The Guest List, The Who's Who, The Photographers, The DVD shoot, The Stretch Limos and the list goes on…

On the other hand, 'The Marriage' is often (but not necessarily so), the house, the shelter, a place where there is going to be lots of "What's for dinner darling?"

So you are best advised to ensure, you are both on the same page when taking that bold step into the unknown.

There is room, in fact, there is need, for both gender perspectives; as one is needed to counterbalance the other…so work together guys… it's about a 'you and I' as well as an 'as well' formula; and not about 'my' ideas 'instead of' yours….

To assist your understanding of the process, one of my lady researchers sent me the following 'Barometer Reading' Chart, which, she advises, that, 'all women' understand; and also provides questions that men in general should memorise, especially during "that time" of the month, and goes something like this…

DANGEROUS	SAFER	SAFEST
1. What's for dinner"?	Can I help you with dinner?	Where would you like to go for dinner?
2. Are you wearing that?	Wow, you sure look good in brown!	WOW! Look at you!
3. What are you so worked up about?	Could we be overreacting?	Here's my paycheck.
4. Should you be eating that?	You know, there are a lot of apples left.	Can I get you a piece of chocolate with that?
5. What did you DO all day?	I hope you didn't over-do it today.	I've always loved you in that robe!

Never mind we seem to be treading on "sensi-tive grounds" here but, I suspect, it is far better to "argue with the Book" than go starting up an 'al-beit unintended' fight; which will in all respects, be a losing battle..

So guys, it's about creating awareness and ap-pealing to your "female" sensitivity, as, like myself, we often don't have "a clue" in such matters.

CHAPTER SEVEN (7)

Cheating Hearts

A S ALLUDED TO EARLIER, what a man 'high on testosterone' may see as a mere "romantic escapade", 'having some fun', 'passing the time', a 'one night stand', call it what you will; a woman, on the other hand, sees it as laying the foundation for a "long term relationship", building her nest, finding her man, her prince charming... it is part of their "DNA" and is automatically and instinctively so..

To put it more succinctly, women in the main, tend to perceive "ownership" with Sex, while men on the other hand ... well... just see "sex" often as an end in itself!!

So, with implications for the creation and survival of the next generation resting biologically on her shoulders, her analysis of the situation has far more ramifications, than the "boo" or "hunk" (we guys in other words), might have realized.

She is in it, for the long haul, as we say...

The question is often asked, "Why do men cheat?" (Ok, I know women cheat as well, but that is for another day – the 'old goose and gander' story)...

Frankly, I believe, that in the majority of cases, men never perceive their pursuits as 'cheating', but more of a 'hunting pleasure', horizontal (or vertical), entertainment, much akin to the emotional level required in roller skating, horse or car racing, taking a long walk, partying all night, or even having 'beers out with the guys'.

It's more of an 'exhilarating' solution to the testosterone drive, which needs to be satisfied, without a second thought of any one else; or even being aware, that anyone else is, or may be, getting emotionally traumatised, in the pursuit of their 'secret addiction'; and the so called bachelors "right of passage".

In fact, having already lived well over a half century of my life, I learned for the first time, mainly through the 'outpourings' of female friends and relatives, that I even began to comprehend, that something "traumatic" occurs in the minds and hearts of our female counterparts, when men do what they think men ought to do... No perhaps without realising it, you're being a "cheat!!"

That's the long and short of what "she" thinks...

One lady met me on the streets downtown one day, and pleaded with me to "talk to her husband for her", asking him to stop seeing, "that other woman", he was apparently seeing.

Her distraught condition, as she made her appeal to me, brought home the notion, that, 'something serious', in so far as she was concerned, was going down, never mind that I could not see how I was going to make contact with 'her man', and invite him to make 'vertical' adjustments to his 'horizontal affairs', as she was pleading with me to do...

Most Men just don't think along those lines, let alone know how to handle stuff like that.

Hey, the guy, if I attempted to approach him, would most likely consider he had every right to let me know, in no uncertain terms, that it was 'none of my damn business', and, depending on his 'intellectual standing', would either, fire carefully crafted expletives, or perceive me, as the latest downtown moron, or worst still, 'I'd become public enemy number one!'

In response to her "How can he do this to me" question, I tried to advance the consolation, that I did not think, that he was thinking, he was doing something to her (on purpose), but I would see how best I could make contact with and talk to him.

Lets hope he eventually gets a copy of this book, as to be quite honest, I still have not yet got the nerve, to phone up the guy, or to check where he hangs out, so I could convey the 'malignant emotion' of his estranged partner.

Maybe some form a "counseling" service, of some sort, is needed here; at the "Institutional" level... so listen up you Governmental agencies...

With every passing encounter of this kind, I have become more and more convinced, that, 'The sexes (are) opposite', to borrow a line from one of the poems, in my earlier poetry titled: '55 Sensations'.

No, you will not be learning that Malcolm just got gunned down in a bar for interfering with other 'big men's business', so please ladies, let him read the Book - hey, I will even offer to help pay for the postage.

I have no interest in passing myself off as some clinical psychologist, but I am "authoritatively" informed, that, at about the age of puberty, there is a left brain/right brain "thing" that goes on in humans; where both sides of the male brain go for the 'logics' compartment (which we alluded to in Chapter One), while the female brain is divided into one side 'logic' and the other side 'caring and sensitivity'.

Before you start the accusation that Malcolm is "just here trying to justify the guys actions with his brain side baloney", (if you would bear with me just for a moment), I would take you through the process, which I've been trying to grapple with, over many years, well past my 50th Birthday; before I would even begin to find, the "radio station" wave band, that my lady friends (target group), were almost instinctively tuned in to, on a full time basis.

I recall hearing some years ago, of a book written by a Trained Clinical Psychologist (whose name currently eludes me…sorry sir), titled: "Men are from Mars and Women from Venus", and quite frankly, did not go out to buy a copy, because I considered, then, that the name of the book had said it all, and as such, was of itself, a "statement of fact", just like that; requiring no further reading!

To be quite honest, that is often the typical male response, unless and until, someone whom we really trust, is able to spell it out for us; in simple and non threatening terms, we proceed in total oblivion, as to why, exactly, the mental 'planets' of the genders are, ostensibly, so far apart.

Then there was this fellow (unknown to me), who 'out out of the blue', walked up and started a conversation with me again downtown one Saturday morning, on my way to or from clearing my Post Office Box....

At first, he appeared to be, (or so I thought, based on previous experience), on the 'prowl' for a monetary 'hand out' - what with his story of how "he was out of work, because somebody at his workplace had 'messed him up', and how he was broke, and was looking for another job, but needed 'something' to help keep him going meanwhile"... I am sure you've heard it all...

I was just beginning to process, in my mind, possible options I would suggest he might consider; i.e. offering his services as a 'floating handyman' to the downtown stores, visiting with the Ministry of Social Services, The Labour Office, the Short Term Employment Programme or equivalent agencies, and the like; when again, out of the blue, he blurted out a totally unexpected statement, as he said: "anyway at least my girlfriend has nice 'tot-tots' (breasts), and that's what's 'keeping me up' for now – if it wasn't for that, I am not sure what I would be doing now… maybe I would be in prison."

At this point, I too became puzzled as to what to say next to this fellow, and, while I am certainly not averse to appreciating a lovely pair on the female form, I was at a loss as to his analogy of "beautiful breasts" being a solution for "unemployment" - but my friends, that was what the man said, and we shortly, thereafter, ended our conversation..

On reflection, I suppose he meant that the breasts of his significant other, were a form of distraction (or attraction), a diversion, or a comfort from the otherwise hardships he was going through.

If, that was the case, then good for him… Far better than joining the 'crime scene' and finishing up in prison, as he had alluded to!

Ladies: just what would we guys do without you?

My only concern thereafter, based upon his logic, was for the young lady in question, whom I thought, would now have to make darn sure that she retains the quality of the physical attributes she possessed, otherwise, would he be back in the market for an alternative pair of "nice tot-tots??"

What I do know, is that the logics of 'why men cheat', has the potential to hold no boundaries in the international game of love and marriage, where "Special Conditions Apply".

"Instead of", is therefore a state of mind, the female mind that is, and seems to sit at the heart of the apparent disparity, between male and female thought, where matters of 'the heart' are concerned.

Ever notice, when in majority of cases where women cheat, barring economic or even physical needs, it is less about 'horizontal entertainment' than it is about 'revenge!'

The "You did it to me – I will do it to you back", 'Eye for an Eye', sort of approach that emerges, and everything is down hill from there, till the limits of emotional and financial exhaustion are reached??

So guys, it would do us a world of good, to at least be aware, that something far larger than what we see as 'entertainment', is attached to the "roving eye"….well!… not the "eye" so much, as "another roving part" of the male anatomy!!…

Nature has so programmed our female counterparts with a strong sense of <u>nest building</u> and <u>ma-</u>

<u>ternal instinct</u>, and anything that remotely appears to encroach on that space, is naturally perceived as 'a threat', and you have to agree, when you can think it out in those terms, it makes a 'heck' of a lot of sense.

Having said that, my dear gentlemen, the concept then seems to play some serious havoc with your own 'sexual prowess', - as you too, soon become so aware of the phenomenon, to the extent that "guilt trips" begin to creep into your own thought process every time a 'sexy chick' chances by; because once married, you too know (or are expected to know), that "external horizontal entertainment", is legally out of bounds, unless guys, it is confined to 'window shopping' only!!!

Not too long ago, Sarah Peter, Editor of the "Youth Oriented" (YO!) Magazine, of The Voice Newspaper in my hometown, put the question in her 'Street Vibes' column to young persons in her readership, and I now invite you to take a look at what 'the Youth' of the day had to say…

The question Ms Peter put to her "research sample" was:

"Can a man romantically fall in love with 'two' women at the same time or vice versa?"

She cautioned, that the answer may not seem as straight forward as you may think it is, and went on to say: "Well, at least that's what I found out, when I posed the question to some of my colleagues and other individuals."

She goes on: "The answers I received to this question were generally and interestingly spilt, with some saying "NO!", "Impossible", "Never", - while others, generally, gave a resounding "YES" to this same question!"

The men with the "YES" response generally contended, that if one can love their sister and mother at the same time, why can't they do the same with two other women? They further attempted to strengthen their arguments, by stating that polygamy does exist in some cultures, and that there is no "switch" on your emotional gate; for one partner over the other.

The male argument continues that suggests its "Okay, as there is only so much love to go around, and you can't only spend it, on one person."

In contrast, some of the girls/women interviewed, stated that an individual cannot really be deeply in love with two people at the same time.

They insisted, that there <u>must be a preference</u>, and while they have acknowledged, that one can be emotionally attached to, or be in lust with, or even be infatuated with, two women at the same time, love for two women simultaneously??.... "Well that's Impossible" - as one interviewee vehemently pointed out.

During the interview, Young Darin stated his position, that "Loving two women at the same time? I do not see any problem in that, because a man, or women for that fact, does not tell his/her heart whom to love, and how many people to have certain feelings for. I can love one woman and love another in the same way, because I might be seeing her at different times of the day."

Perhaps "Darin" was giving the 'typical' young male response... no holes barred!!...

On the other hand, "Merlin" held firmly to the view that, "You cannot be in love with two women at the same time. Romantic love is a once in a lifetime thing, and it takes your whole heart to love someone deeply, truly, honestly, and with respect."

"Besides" she continues, "if you get emotionally attached to, or in lust with etc., you might care for one and love the other; but it will not be true deep love for both at the same time. Furthermore, between the two women, there will always be one of them you will have that special connection with."

Merlin, in my view, gives the true and again unadulterated 'Instead of' response; typical of the "generic" female mind…she's not wrong guys, just different.

Along comes Charlene and further reinforces the "female" perspective even further, when she said: "I believe that both sexes can have attractions for two people, but in my opinion, for one of them, it would have to be lust and not love. Moreover, I believe, you can only have one true, deep feeling, for just one person."

The "logic" of Paul kicks in when he says: "Well I think so. Love is not a finite commodity. Loving one person doesn't necessarily diminish your love for the other. I love my brothers in the same way, so why can't I love two girls at the same time? - there is nothing wrong with that!"

Alice again begs to differ, in that, "To love two women at the same time may not necessarily be right, but that's one of the things that one does not have any control over, because, probably, what the man is looking for, he might not find it in one woman, and it might be the same for the woman. And yes, a woman can also be in love with two men at the same time, nonetheless, women are able to make a more concrete decision and just choose one person ultimately. On the other hand, men will juggle the two, until their secret is discovered."

Just some food for thought as we say, this time coming from the "youth" in our quest for a better understanding of the different thought processes of the male and female minds ("now" generation or "sensible" seniors); neither of whom, most of the time, have the "remotest" clue of the true perspective of the other…

The dilemma that is "Instead of", versus the "As well" factor, is a real one, as we begin to see the dichotomy that exists between the sexes, which instincts, as alluded to earlier, continue to sit at the heart of marital disparities the world over.

Coming to grips with the reality, and understanding the dichotomy, cannot hurt…and I reiterate, it is NOT about who is right or wrong…you are both right, and perhaps both wrong, in the natural order of things…What counts here is the "awareness and sensitivity" to the differences…a heck of a lot of "intellectual helium", (hot air), could be saved, by preventing proverbial arguments in the first place, across the planet…

The pages of this book would not be complete, if I did not "infuse" an aspect of the "Biblical perspective" as, I certainly believe, that if we rely purely on our own strengths and genius, we would ultimately fall "flat on our faces".

One International Pastor, Dr John Hagee, in his "Life Study Plan Bible", talks of the concept of "forgiveness and the Freedom that is associated with it", and tells the story of how, late one night, he had a phone call and heard somebody sobbing on the other end of the line, and I quote:

"It was a dear friend, whose wife of many years had just told him that she was divorcing him."

"By her own confession, he was a loyal husband and an excellent provider, but she had been having an office affair and was in love with the other man. She took the children and moved to another State, leaving the broken hearted man, to a silent house full of memories."

"His emotional nightmare affected, not only his job performance, but his friends also withdrew from him."

Pastor advised the gentleman, that he must forgive his wife completely saying "If you don't forgive her, you are going to live the rest of your life, in an emotional penitentiary, to which she is going to hold the keys; and she will be your master and tormenter, until you forgive her."

Dr Hagee advocates that: "the secret formula called "forgiveness" is apparently not for the other person's benefit, but rather for your benefit."

So go ahead, start forgiving that "demon" in the 'guy next door' in order to release your own freedom, as "there is said to be freedom in forgiveness".

No harm in giving the concept a try, and if you are really into Bible readings, go ahead, the good Pastor says, and turn to Jeremiah 14:19…

So there you are… Bet you did not expect to be at the receiving end of a good "bible lesson" in the intriguing subject of this Chapter.

IS SHE CHEATING?

The following lines are taken from an article written by Steve Calechman from Men's Health (lifestyle.msn. com), for those of you who may need pointers to help you determine when to be concerned, where the writer says, and I quote:

"You have a great gal. So great, in fact, that she attracts packs of men who try to capture her attention, or worse, coax her out of her clothes. They could be platonic friends, or they could be interlopers, scourges, bent on emasculating and circumventing you. What to do?"

"Everything starts with having ground rules, open communication, and strategies for how to proceed" - says Janice Levine, Ph.D., a psychologist in Lexington, Massachusetts, and the author of *"Why Do Fools Fall in Love?"* Either blowing your lid or turning a blind eye could create more problems than addressing the situation head-on.

Dr Levine suggests the following tips, that will help you know if there are signs of cheating wife or girlfriend, and indeed, to help you stand your ground, without devolving into a raging (soon to be single) maniac!!...

Check out the following areas...

• **THE OVERLY INTERESTED BOSS AT WORK**

Worry when ... she's focused on pleasing him, not doing her job.

Not when ... "he's a kindhearted mentor. His motives could be sincere, and, if she's happy at work, she'll be happy at home", says Jeffrey Bernstein, Ph.D., another psychologist, and the author of *"Why Can't You Read My Mind?"*

Your move, as suggested, is to "Lead with concern for her, not your issues. If she thinks you have an agenda, she'll become defensive and fail to see any negatives, just to prove you wrong." Say for example "It seems your boss is really helping you. How's that going?"

• THE EX SHE'S STILL FRIENDS WITH

Worry when... they talk frequently and secretly. Regular contact sends up flares. Covertness fires a cannon.

Not when... she has a once-a-year, 15-minute phone call. There's a lot of history— some good.

Your move: Calmly say, "I have a problem with the relationship, because I don't understand it. Can you tell me what it does for you?" suggests Jackie Jaye Brandt, M.F.T., a psychotherapist in Universal City, California. You're not being invasive, you're just gathering information. An ultimatum leads to resentment— or abandonment. Be ready to walk out the door if she picks him.

• THE EX SHE STILL PINES FOR

Worry when... she drops his name in subtle or obvious comparisons to you. If he initiated the breakup, there's a big chance she's holding on to the fantasy.

Not when... it might be just fond memories, so the threat could be all in your head.

Your move: Say, "I just need some reassurance here." She should respond definitively that you're her man, Levine says. If she pauses, follow up with "I'm not trying to control you. I just want to be with someone who knows what she wants." She needs to think it's something to fix. If she doesn't... Walk!!

- ## THE HANDS-ON PERSONAL TRAINER

Worry when... she spills intimate details about his life. Chances are the sharing goes both ways. "The relationship should be friendly, not familiar" says Rita De Maria, Ph.D., a marriage and family therapist in the Philadelphia area.

Not when... he's just pumping her up. It's his job to give her encouragement and attention.

Your move: Once again, share your discomfort and watch her response. If she's open and says "I didn't realise that", she's not drinking in the man's attention, and she respects your feelings. If she's defensive, she might be guzzling it, so back off for a few weeks and see how she deals with it. It's up to you how far you push.

* THE SMITTEN SUITOR

Worry when... she's ignoring the situation because she hates conflict. That's bad for your relationship, because this issue will recur.

Not when... she's simply working at her own pace to let her admirer down easy.

Your move: If you've given her pace a chance, let her know you're uncomfortable. Offer to help. If she allows you, meet the guy; put your arm around her, and introduce yourself as her boyfriend. That should be enough. If it's not, say "I think it would be best if you limited contact with her" Levine says. "Use restrained strength, not tough-guy tactics."

Unquote

The foregoing thoughts "borrowed" from the writers as stated, brings an international dimension to the theme and considerations of the varied components of adult relationships...

While we respect the opinions of the "experts" (and I would encourage you to read up on as many of their texts as may be available to you), remember, that your own success, or failure, in this delicate field, is predicated only upon your own ability to internalise the concepts, and adopt and adapt them into your own domestic situation...

There is no "one size fits all" situation - a Caribbean perspective is different from a North American, European or Far Eastern perspective; in much the same way, as each household and each individual case, must be decided upon based on its own merit!

CHAPTER EIGHT (8)

Bill of Rights

A**S THE PREVIOUS LINES** would by now have attested, you can't win, (easily), in this business of "romance" and all of its associated nuances.

To be anywhere near successful though, you just have to 'roll with the punches' and hey, I don't mean that literally, lest I be accused of promoting some "subtle" form of domestic violence!

No, the idea as far as I see it, is to try to 'go with the flow'...

Guys, when your lady comes up with an idea, a proposal, which to you, sounds like something that just sprung to her mind, you are wrong if you feel you can simply dismiss it ...take it from me...

The lady has literally "sat up all night" thinking this thing through, and will do all in her power to convince you, even if not at that time, but later on, when she thinks the "timing is right".

She will create "the right times", and before you know it, she has you hooked on the idea, that you unknowingly, and even willingly, proceed to buy into; never mind your earlier attempts at dismissing the matter.

It would be a recipe for another argument if you failed to comply! Which subject, just to lighten up, I consider, calls for a bit of 'couples humour' on arguments between the genders where, 'Once upon a time' so the story goes...Quote:

A man and his wife were having an argument in bed. After the husband had finally had enough, he jumped up and took a blanket to the couch. The next day, the wife feeling badly about what happened, decided to buy her husband a gift.

Since he was an avid Golfer, she went to the Pro Shop at the Club where he usually played golf. The wife talked with the Pro, and he suggested a putter and showed her one of his finest. "How much is it?" she asked. "One hundred and fifty dollars" he replied. She felt that was kind of expensive, so she told him so.

"But it comes with an inscription" the pro said. "What kind of inscription?" she asked. "Whatever you wish" he explained. "But, one of the old golfers' favourites is 'Never Up, Never In'".

"Oh, that will never do!" exclaimed the wife. "That's what started the argument in the first place!!" Unquote.

Ah well, hope it at least gives you a chuckle……

I was again reading the other day, where a lady writer from Salt Lake City Utah, by the name of Jill Adler, who loves researching relationships, and who had drafted her own suggested "Bill of Rights" - as she says, for the "Wives of America".

She says in her preamble, and again I quote:

"We, the wives of America, love being married to the husbands of America. We know we have our faults, but with ever-morphing roles these days, there's a lot of pressure on us 'to be superhuman'. We care for our families, manage the home, keep ourselves attractive, and even bring home our share of the bacon. We know we sometimes lash out, but we really do want to 'live happily ever after' with you. Our mutual acknowledgement of these proposed amendments can go a long way toward achieving that."

She has therefore produced the following "Declaration of Amendments".

The Wife's Bill of Rights

(As drafted By Jill Adler)

- **Amendment I**
  We have the right to dislike your buddies.
  We know it's important for you to have your guy friends, but you should know by now, that we're not turned on by your stories, of the good old days at College, your sexual exploits, or which relief pitcher the Red Sox should trade. Disappear for a while and be boys – its ok, go chug beer and high-five – but please don't expect us to be happy when your friends come over, and put their feet on our coffee tables, or leave their beer cans on the floor.

- <u>**Amendment II**</u>
<u>**We have the right to experience 'PMS' in all its glory.**</u>
Either give us our space or accept the consequences. We know it's unfair, but some of us just can't rein it in. You knew that before you married us. We may shout, cry, belittle, and act irrationally. It lasts just a few days each month, so please deal with it. Or even better: Bring home dinner, clear the dishes, and give us a big hug.

- <u>**Amendment III**</u>
<u>**We have the right to demand, that you finish a household job.**</u>
We're not your mother, and we loathe having to act like them. If you wash the dishes, do them all and clean the sink, too. Don't just bag the trash; take it outside to the bin. If you start a load of laundry, put it in the dryer and fold it too. We don't like nagging, anymore than you like hearing it.

- <u>**Amendment IV**</u>
<u>**We have the right to an honest answer to "What is wrong?"**</u>
We admit guilt in this area too, but "Nothing" says nothing. If we ask it's not because we're trying to make a casual conversation. It's because we love you and need an honest answer. If there truly is nothing wrong, then ask why

we think otherwise. Yes, this could open a can of worms, but remember the time when we dated, and talked about everything?

- **Amendment V**
  We have the right to keep our secrets.
  Not marriage-ending ones, just small secrets we choose to hide from others. If we don't want to speak our age or share our true hair colour, or reveal the 'cheesy TV shows' we watch in private, it's not your place to reveal them to our friends, your business partners, or your ex-girlfriends/wives. We're not asking you to lie for us, but we would appreciate your discretion.

- **Amendment VI**
  We have the right to clean air.
  You may think its funny, masculine, or natural, to pass gas anywhere and anytime you please, but when the smell drives us to gag, it's uncool. There is something inherently wrong in the relationship, if you must walk over to us and fart, or if you intentionally set a bad example for the kids. We fart too, but we do so discreetly for a reason. You may not like our potpourri and scented candles, but they're infinitely better, than toxic and flammable methane!

- **Amendment VII**
  We have the right to keep and bear tons of girly bathroom products.
  You have your tools; so do we. These items are expensive and are to be used sparingly. It brings no joy to see our $15 bath soap bar, shrunk down to the size of a quarter, after two passes on your chest and legs.

- **Amendment VIII**
  We have the right to speak to our girlfriends everyday.
  About whatever we want, whenever we want. Please don't eavesdrop or criticise. We know you're not that interested in gossip or psycho-analytical interpretations, of why some people do what they do, so we turn to our like-minded female friends for instant gratification. Yes, we do talk about you – a lot. It helps us work through issues. This keeps us happy, sane and; usually, off your case.

- **Amendment IX**
  We have the right to flirt.
  Not the kind that makes you jealous; but the healthy practice of connecting with another person; on a non-sexual level. Light banter is fun, quick-witted, and encouraging to our self esteem. It might even remind you of why you fell in love with us. And if it gets us a "smoking" deal on that new furnace; or a free stay for

the family, (at a million dollar ski chalet); so much the better.

- **<u>Amendment X</u>**
  <u>We have the right to foreplay.</u>
  A fine bottle of wine, soft music, deep looks into each other's eyes, compliments holding hands, cuddling - these are all forms of foreplay. And, we insist on them. Please don't reach for our crotch or breasts and expect us to "melt into a porn kitten". It didn't work when we met, it most certainly doesn't work now. Sure, we women are strong and independent, and appreciate an inspired 'quickie' when the moment strikes; but we also have an inner soft spot (the size of Texas), that needs sharing and cherishing. We appreciate you more, when you think about how it feels to us, rather than how it feels to you.

She concludes with the question "tell us" ladies... Would you add or remove any 'rights' from this list?

Not to be outdone, in response to the forgoing declaration, a "brave fellow" by the name of Craig Playstead, from the 'Surburbs of Seattle', has sought to put forward his own list, which he calls "<u>The Husbands' of Bill Rights</u>", and in his preamble proclaims to us that, quote:

"We, the husbands of America, do not claim to be perfect. We're far from it. While we love being married to the wives of America, we have a few things that we'd like to straighten out. We're not asking for the world here. We understand, that things like following our College football team, to every away game, is out of the question, as are after-dinner cigars.

However, there are a few minor things that we'd like to clear up, to make our marriage a happy one…Enter…

The Husband's Bill of Rights

By Craig Playstead

- **Amendment I**
  We have the right to go out with our friends at least once a month.
  A man's relationship with his buddies is a bond that should never be broken. It helps keep us feeling young, connected and sane. It also helps us break the routine, just like "nights with the girls" do for you. Even as we reach middle age, we like the fact that we still have a "crew".

- **Amendment II**
  We reserve the right, to dislike your friend's husbands.
  We promise to give the guy a fair shot, but when he starts acting like a moron, we can no longer authorise events with that family. And yes, wives have the same freedom to blackball, when the tables are turned. It doesn't mean we like your friend any less, it just means, that in her haste to have a big, fancy wedding, she chose a 'jackass', whom we don't want to spend our spare time with. Listening to stories about how "wicked" he was, on the French horn, in his "bitchin' 80s band", is just too much!

- **Amendment III**
  We have the right, to have a few things of ours in the house.
  Everything we hold near and dear to us, shouldn't all be in the garage. While we un-

derstand, that our framed "Kiss Concert Poster", might not make it on the living room wall, at least throw us a bone. The scene in "Juno" where Jason Bateman realised, that everything he held near and dear, was in a 200-square-foot room, was a gut-shot to us all.

- **Amendment IV**
  We have the right NOT to be scolded by you.
  We are your husbands, not your children. We don't mean to track dirt onto the carpet, or get chips on the couch; but it's not like we just got a lap dance. Don't treat us like your children, and we'll do our best not to act like them.

- **Amendment V**
  We have the right to teach our sons, how to "pass gas" in manly form (of course, this varies according to local culture....).
  Sharing bodily functions with our offspring, is much about life, as it is about jokes. It's also something that can help bring kids and dads together. Believe me, kids and guys always laugh at farts - that's how we're wired. And we're not talking about being totally gross and inappropriate. We vow to teach them, that there is a time, and a place, for behavior like this; and that the early service at Church, is not one of them.

- **Amendment VI**
  We have the right to teach our children how to defend themselves.
  Fighting is barbaric, terrible, and scary. But it's also part of growing up. We want our kids, to be able to get out of a bad situation, not be bullied, and to be able to take care of themselves. One of the plus sides of learning how to take care of yourself, is that the more you know, the less you have to use it. Teaching our offspring, how to defend themselves, in a scary world, is one of the basic duties of a father.

- **Amendment VII**
  We have the right, to as much reading material in the bathroom, as we need.
  Sometimes we're in there for a quite while, can't help it. And no, we're not hiding… most of the time.

- **Amendment VIII**
  We have the right to watch the big game.
  We care too much about our teams. We know it's not rational, but it's who we are. No one can explain, the love men have for their teams, but you may as well embrace it, because that love will not die. If you don't believe this, just remember the "Boston Red Sox" had the most loyal fans in sport, and didn't win a World Series for 86 years.

- **Amendment IX**
  We have the right to the "remote", when we're on the couch.
  This is something that is in our DNA. - We know it, and you know it. If there is any doubt, watch us 'surf' at top speed, while knowing if a show is worth watching after stopping on it for just '2 seconds'. It's a thing of beauty....

- **Amendment X**
  We have the right to still use chivalry.
  Yes ... we know women are strong and inde-pendent, and we 'dig' that, but allow us to open the door for you, or give up a seat and act like a gentleman; once in a while. The world will be a better place because of it.

Let's hear it guys:

Would you add or remove any 'rights' from this list?

(N.B: Craig Playstead is a freelance writer and a happily married father of three, living in the sub-urbs of Seattle. In the past he's also been a sports writer, online editor, and a talk show host. You can reach him at playstead@hotmail.com for additional information)

The above writings have emanated from "research" by the above in a US based setting...

And now, to add my own "two cents"...

The seemingly light hearted 'banter' (set out in a humourous format), that these 'Bills of Rights' are intended to convey, to my own mind, also represent the 'cry' out between the sexes, for greater understanding, compassion and empathy between them.

Both genders… repeat both genders…therefore need to exhibit greater sensitivity to each others wants, desires and needs.

The problem to my mind, is, that it is often a matter of both "sides" making incorrect assumptions about what the other might actually need; and like the rest of us, remain in 'romantic limbo' for decades on end, before discovering, or realising, the simple 'do's and don'ts'.

And so in my next Chapter, I am going to invite a lady professional, for whom I have come to have very high regard, for her efforts to inform her local Caribbean community, over the many years…

CHAPTER NINE (9)

Let's be Gender Sensitive

A s I said, this time round, I'm "gonna" be needing lots of help, from my friends of the opposite gender.

In attempting to produce a Chapter that makes a lot of good and balanced sense, I've got to have some serious 'female' input, and as I have already admitted to, I still don't have a 'clue', as far as "answers", at comprehending the minds of the opposite gender are concerned.

To top it up, any answers that I might think I have been able to figure out, would I am sure, have to pass the test of other variables; including menstrual cycles, PMS, hot flashes, and a host of other yet unexplained phenomena; well outside of my "male" comprehension. (Yes, here he goes again you say, here he goes again!!)

Yes, I have read where certain chemicals in the brain, such as Dopamin, Oxytosin and Vaso-'something', are responsible for 'making decisions', of which I know little about.

So I will call and see how willing, and I am sure, more than able, this lady doctor friend of the family is; to shed some light on the subject of helping us men, to become gender sensitive.

My dear family friend, Dr. Marie Grandison - Didier, Medical Practitioner and Dermatologist by profession, and a long standing Community Counsellor writes ....

ON THE CHANGING FACE OF MALE FEMALE INTERACTION AND BEAUTY IN THE LATE 20TH AND EARLY 21ST CENTURY

It took many months to finally get started on this chapter. At first (as we so often do), I thought that this would be a fairly straight forward undertaking. As the enormity of the subject began to settle on the rational side of my mind, I realised that, this would require enormous effort, to try to distil out the complexities of the changes which have taken place. To a large extent, I will speak from the Caribbean perspective, but will attempt to bring whatever scientific, or other evidence, to bear; as seems relevant.

My perspective on the subject will be coloured by all the factors which have exerted an influence on making me the person who I am today. These factors include my gender, religious beliefs, schooling, culture, the time period in which I grew up, important persons who had an impact on my life and many others.

Having been born in the mid 20th century I would like to classify myself as a young, but aging baby boomer. I am old enough to have sung along with Mitch Miller and the gang; but young enough to appreciate the music of John Legend, Rihanna and Beyonce. I can therefore, truly say, that my perspective on the subject is a multi generational one.

As a medical doctor in this 21st century, in which the watchword of "evidence based", is the gold standard to which we must adhere, I thought it prudent, to first look at the biological basis of male female interaction as science understands it today; and then to look at what it appears to be obtaining in our Caribbean area. Finally, I will advance my own opinion based on my interactions with patients in my twenty-five years as a physician (nineteen of which, have been spent in one or other area of sexually transmitted diseases), as to the factors which have precipitated the changes which we are seeing.

A phenomenal amount of research is currently being done into the factors which appear to influence the attraction between males and females. We hold that we are creatures of higher intelligence who make decisions based on higher thought processes and not on instinct and primal drives; yet, with the greater advances in medical knowledge, we have become more aware that there is a considerable amount of genetically predetermined hard wiring, which may exert significant influence over the factors which determine whom we are attracted to as a partner. No researcher is suggesting that we are all purely pheromone driven; but certainly there appears to be a subliminal genetic drum beat, to which we may all be marching.

Two of the very interesting bodies of work on attraction of the opposite sex to each other, center on the role which 'odour', and the perception of how a person of the opposite sex smells, affects choice of a partner. These are independent studies, being done by groups in universities on opposite sides of the Atlantic, yet they are making determinations and advancing postulates, based on objective evidence, which appears to link perception of odour, with our reaction to members of the opposite sex.

In a collaborative study done by Duke University in North Carolina and Rockefeller University in New York, an odorant receptor ORD7D4, has been identified. This receptor, determines how we perceive the odour produced under the influence of the hormone Androstenedione (a male hormone). Some persons perceive the odour to be pleasant, (akin to vanilla), while others perceive the odour to be offensive, (akin to urine). The avenues which are now being explored are those to find the gene which codes for ORD7D4 and the gene which codes for the levels of Androstenedione in the body. The postulate from this research would tend to suggest that depending on how much of the hormone we produce and the perception of its smell by the person we are interacting with, there may be a genetically determined, positive, or negative, response.

An even more compelling study has been done by a collaborative group in the United Kingdom. The University of Liverpool and the University of Newcastle have looked together at the similarities and differences in the immune systems of men and women, and how attractive, or unattractive, they find each other's body odour. The evidence, thus far, suggests that the more dissimilar the immune systems of a man and a woman are, the more attractive they find each other's body odour. They have done this work looking at the MHC (major histocompatability complex) marker.

Two conclusions have, thus far, come from this work. The first is that a man and woman, with very similar MHC markers, may have fertility problems; and the second is, that a child born to these persons may not have as efficient an immune system, and thus, be more prone to illness. This research would tend to suggest, that pre-programmed in our genetic make up, is the ability to choose a mate who would, when our genes combine, produce children with the best chance of survival. "Survival of the fittest" as Darwin postulated, would be promoted by these combinations of genes.

Perhaps the most interesting part of this research is the suggestion that, the oral contraceptive pill causes women to find the odour of men with genetically similar immune systems attractive. This reverses the response normally seen. The effect of this reversal in attraction, mediated by the oral contraceptive pill, would be to remove the genetically mediated protection for fertility. The immunological well being of the baby, could also, possibly, be compromised.

Even more thought provoking, is the possibility, that a woman might meet a man while on the pill, find him attractive, settle down with him, decide to have a baby, stop the pill, and then find him unattractive! The permutations and combinations here provide much food for thought.

A study, done by N. Pipitone and G. Gallop at the State University of New York, has shown that men respond more positively, and are more attracted to, women at the time of ovulation. This is not only manifested in attraction to the facial features (the lips look fuller and the faces look more flushed), but even in non-visual cues such as the attractiveness of the sound of the voice. Women were recorded counting from one to ten in a non-ovulatory part of the menstrual cycle, and the ovulatory part of the cycle. I think we would all agree that a brisk count from one to ten would hardly be classified as the world's most sexy recording. Men found the voices in the ovulatory part of the cycle more attractive. Given that this is her most fertile period, this would be an adaptation to facilitate survival of the species, as she would be more desirable at that time, and the male would be more likely to have sexual desire for her.

Despite the fact that we have no overt displays, like some species of apes, and no massive pheromone release, like a female dog; we do seem to have poorly recognised, and even more poorly understood, subliminal messages, which we are sending and receiving on a daily basis. These messages may not be the principal guiding force in our attraction to each other, but they may provide subtle cues in determining our final choice of a mate.

As we look around the world, we realise that the standards of beauty vary greatly in the more primitive cultures. The tribal scarification of some African tribes, (which make the average person in a western culture cringe), or the neck elongation of other tribes, clearly indicate, that in isolated communities, standards develop independently, and are maintained when no external influence is exerted.

With the advent of mass telecommunications and the pervasive cultural penetration of western (largely American), values globally, there has been a frame shift in what is accepted as the standard of beauty, and further, what is accepted as the norm.

In the late nineteen sixties, and the early nineteen seventies, in the Caribbean, one was considered on the cutting edge, and bordering on avant-garde, if one placed a second hole in one's ear! This second piercing carried a possible negative connotation with respect to one's morality. In fact the view held at that time, was that such an act was carried out, by ladies who practiced the world's oldest profession. Equally (or perhaps more so), wearing an anklet was the ultimate sign of moral decadence.

It is now absolutely acceptable and considered an enhancement of beauty to have multiple piercing, and piercing in places which certainly seem more likely to be injurious to health, rather than an aid to beauty!

In my time in the sexually transmitted disease clinics, I have witnessed a new trend in male piercing. This is the insertion of ball bearings under the foreskin of the male penis just below the coronal sulcus. The coronal sulcus being the area which is just below the head of the penis and at the lower end of the penile shaft. This activity seems to be more common in those who operate in the murky realm of illegal activities and even more so in "gentlemen" who have at some time, been at "Her Majesty's Pleasure".

When I politely enquired about the purpose of the addition, I was advised that this was to facilitate the enhanced pleasure of their sexual partner. I have not yet managed to get the opinion of any of the recipients of this revved up equipment.

Another interesting change in beauty standards, which has occurred, is the absolute explosion in the application of tattoos. A significant percentage of my patients in the twenty to twenty five year age group, have, at least, one tattoo, and some have multiple tattoos. In St. Lucia, we now have several tattoo parlours (something which was unheard of in the early nineteen nineties), and even a traveling tattoo artist who will do 'in home' consultations. Most of this trend, in permanent self change, stems from the exposure of our youth to the American rap/hip-hop culture. The majority of the rap artists have multiple tattoos. Many of the basketball players, whom they idolise, are also similarly embellished.

A curious change which has taken place in the standards of beauty in recent times has been the change from subtle enhancement to blatant excessive falsehood. Interestingly, the "blatant excessive falsehood" is becoming the accepted standard in many quarters. This I would term the "Dolly Parton/Pamela Anderson Factor". These women have had breast implants, which were massively excessive and undeniably false.

We now view the talon like finger nails, which render the hands dysfunctional and possibly a health hazard, as eminently beautiful and desirable. One can only imagine the number of germs which can find safe harbour under these nails. As a physician, one of the most important activities we practice is hand washing, and close attention is placed on cleaning the nails before surgical procedures.

I viewed with a combination of amazement and amusement, sets of false toenails on sale at a local pharmacy. The toenails are yet another addition to our armamentarium of falsehood.

We now see the improbably long hair extensions, as the sine qua non of beauty. In every small boutique, department store and pharmacy, many square feet of shelf space are dedicated to a dizzying selection of "hair". One can only speculate as to the source of this apparently inexhaustible supply of supposedly human hair. There is now a new acronym H.I.B. (this stands for Hair I Bought).

In the true spirit of West Indian irreverence, and tongue in cheek humour, an advertisement appeared on television in St. Lucia which stated: "Why grow, when you can buy?"

It is a curious paradox that, despite the fact the gold standard for extensions and wigs, is that they should be made from human hair; your wig does not have to fulfill the criterion of even pretending to appear natural. In fact, in the Pasa Pasa subculture of Jamaica, your wig colour should match the colour of your outfit. .

There does appear to be a subtle difference in this perception of what is beautiful, which seems to be governed by educational level and career achievement. The adoption of the managed locks hair style, (the so called sister locks), is much more common in the educated and successful career women, than it is in the lower socio-economic classes. This leads me to wonder, whether a sense of satisfaction with our achievements as black women, allows us to be more comfortable in celebrating our negritude.

Perhaps, the most disconcerting change, which I have seen take place in the standards of beauty in the Caribbean, is the phenomenon of bleaching of the skin to make it lighter in colour.

Having grown up in the post colonial period in Jamaica's history, when a lighter shade of skin was considered a distinct advantage, I then came through the self acceptance and self pride days of the Black power movement. We wore our afros with pride and braided our natural hair. Some of us (including myself), embraced the peaceful approach espoused by Martin Luther King; while others saw Malcolm X and Stokely Carmichael as being their role models for change.

We all wished for an era where we could be accepted for who we were and the natural corollary was that we would accept ourselves.

It was, after all, in Jamaica, (land of my birth), that Rastafarianism, with its paramount message of black pride and black strength, sprung to life in the nineteen thirties. It was Jamaica which gave the world the maverick black thinker Marcus Mosiah Garvey.

How then can we explain, that in the late twentieth century, and progressively so in the twenty-first century, we have seen a disconcerting trend of lightening of the skin with a plethora of agents? How can we explain that this trend was first noted in Jamaica, the cradle of black awareness?

When first reported in a paper presented at the Caribbean Dermatology Association Conference by Dr. Richard Desnoes (a registrar in Dermatology at the University of the West Indies Mona Campus), in the year two-thousand and one; most of us working in other islands of the Caribbean, viewed it as a curious, and quite likely, passing phenomenon.

To our dismay, we have watched this contagion creeping through the Caribbean. Dr. Desnoes has continued his research and presented his latest findings in the year two-thousand and six, in a paper entitled: "The dark side of the bleaching and browning syndrome". This self altering, though more prevalent among females, is also practiced by some males.

A visit to any Pharmacy in St. Lucia, will reveal, a plethora of agents, all dedicated to creating "a lighter brighter complexion".

Could it be, that the cultural penetration of the western television, with its largely Caucasian images, has served to reverse the gains previously made?

This would seem improbable as we still have our Denzel Washingtons, we now have our Morgan Freemans, we have our Will Smiths, and we have our Whoopie Goldbergs and our Oprah Winfreys.

We, in the Caribbean, have given the world the undeniably black and unquestionably beautiful Wendy Fitzwilliam - Ms. Universe 1998. Could it possibly be, that having placed our faith in our black leaders over the past forty years, and having seen our fortunes wane rather than wax, we subconsciously feel that we cannot succeed if we are black?

In fact, if the truth be told, many of our leaders were, in fact, of a lighter hue; perhaps, suggesting that to get to the top, one needed to have a similar colour. Perhaps it is the continuous images of black on black civil war in all its brutality, which makes us yearn to be something other than we are. It appears to me that seemingly endless parade of coups, counter coups, despots and self proclaimed presidents, create a negative self image in us.

The pop culture in Jamaica also reinforces this preference for a lighter skin colour, as the "browning" is revered. A browning being a light skinned female. In St. Lucia the equivalent of a browning is a "chabin".

Despite the fact that we have 'Black History Month' in February, which attempts to instill us with pride in our roots, and to highlight many of the accomplishments of persons of colour, we still do not accept ourselves for what we are. It may take a long time to erase the concept of Africa as the "dark continent", and the idea that its people, and those who issued from that land, are unattractive and barbaric.

Studies have shown that there is a waist to hip ratio which is most attractive to males. This ratio is 0.7 to 1.0. Women with this body shape are said to have high oestradiol levels and are more fertile. An interesting finding in this study, is, that they are more likely to practice serial monogamy, a phenomenon seen in the Caribbean.

There appears to have been a change in the accepted body shape which is considered beautiful. In this regard there has been an acceptance by the first (largely Caucasian) world, of the black female body habitus, in which the gluteal region (the behind), is seen as a desirable and acceptable protuberance on the female body. This new found reverence for the rear has been ascribed to Jennifer Lopez, who has some, not inconsiderable, posterior curves.

It may have escaped the notice of the average shopper, but it is clear that all mannequins designed to display female trousers, now have well endowed posteriors. Not to be out done, there were reports in the daily newspapers in Jamaica, of women taking chicken pills to enhance their upper anterior and lower posterior assets. Here again we see the tendency to exaggerate, to the point of caricature, the new standard of beauty.

In the Caucasian population, other changes in beauty standards are also being seen. Caucasian women are now doing augmentation procedures to make their lips thicker and fuller. This is a full reversal of the trends seen in the early to mid twentieth century, when the thicker Negroid lips were considered unattractive.

It is not only in the female population that there have been changes in the standards that are considered attractive. We have transitioned through the clean cut, neatly clad period of the early twentieth century, to the "wild haired hippy" unkempt period of the sixties. We then had the GQ poster boy male of the seventies, who wore the one diamond stud in his ear, while the seventies also produced, the jerry curled bejeweled pimp look-alike.

In the twenty-first century, we see an eclectic grouping of appearances which are considered attractive. There is less standardization and clone like uniformity in males when one looks across the age-groups. A male sporting Rastafarian locks, may be seen clad in an Armani suit.

This picture is an oxymoron-like juxtaposition, where "natty-dread" meets "Babylon".

Patterned braiding in the hair of a male, which would have been considered decidedly effeminate in the late sixties and early seventies, is now standard fare.

Within the younger males there is a definite gravitation toward the thug appearance. Clothing several sizes too large are a must have. Equally the males wear several layers even in the tropics! As a physician it never fails to amaze me, when I ask a young male patient to undress. His pants will be followed by a pair of shorts, which will be followed by a pair of boxers, which may be followed by a pair of briefs. All this I might add in ninety degree heat! His shirt will be followed by a tee-shirt, which may be followed by a vest!

We must not forget to indicate, that the pants will be defying gravity by clinging precariously to the rear end, while the under pants, suitably emblazoned with a well known brand name, will be exposed for perusal and, it seems, admiration. This is the new standard of "beauty" known as "sagging".

Contrast this if you will, with the request for a young lady to undress. She will be wearing a tiny top two sizes too small, from which her abundant assets are precariously in danger of spilling. She is highly unlikely to be wearing any upper undergarment. Her low rise jeans will have descended to expose her natal cleft as she sits on the chair, and the upper support of her thong (which incidentally matches her blouse), will be clearly visible!

Our young men have drifted away from the multiple chained (Mr. T style) adornment, of the bygone era. They have now adopted the single three-quarter inch wide chain, which hangs down to the upper abdominal area with the mandatory "Jesus Piece" - the latter being an irreverent reference to the cross, which hangs from the chain. Many have also adopted the gang related coloured head-ties, with the reversed baseball cap.

A necessary adjunct to this somewhat disheveled appearance (which is now accepted as attractive for the male), is the need to have a facial expression which can only be described as an intimidating scowl.

The 'piece de resistance' to complete the look, is an improbable gait which will, no doubt, sow the seeds for serious osteoarthritis in the later years.

Whereas, to those of us in the older generation, this young man, as described above, evokes a response of bemused consternation to a young lady of his age group; he represents the epitome of sartorial elegance. In their terms he is "fly".....

We have taken a brief look at some biological factors which may help to govern male female attraction. We have looked at some of the changes in standards of beauty which have occurred during the course of my lifetime. I will now look at some of the sociological factors which act as determinants in the male female attraction.

The course of the twentieth century has chronicled some of the most extensive changes in the sociological framework, in which mankind and, especially, western cultures operate.

There have been significantly changing female roles in society, which appear to have resulted in a paradigm shift in male female relationships.

In his book 'Men at Risk', Professor Errol Miller did exhaustive research. He looked at both developed and developing societies, and the trends seemed to indicate; that, despite the fact that they were starting from widely disparate points, and despite the fact, that there were clearly different variables at work; there has been a progressive drift, (in all the societies studied), towards the same pattern of male female relationship. The common end points seemed to be more single parent homes headed by women and less marriages. It was a widely held premise (here in the Caribbean), that the tendency for fathers to be absent from the family structure, stemmed from our history of slavery.

This premise is now being called into serious question, as a similar trend is seen to be developing in first world countries, where marriage, as an institution, is becoming less popular; and conversely, single parent households, headed by women, more popular.

One of the major factors, which may have contributed to this change, has been the change in the educational levels and occupations of women over the course of the twentieth century.

Miller looked at the occupational profile of women in the USA and deduced, that up to the year nineteen sixty (1960), there were six occupations in which women predominated; and that eighty percent (80%) of women in the workforce of the USA, worked in one of these jobs. The jobs were as follows:

I. Nurses   84%
2. Clerical workers   79%
3. Teachers   77%
4. Textile workers   76%
5. Sales clerks   67%
6. Service workers   62%

Source: Men At Risk Prof. Errol Miller 1995

Even more interesting was the fact that the vast majority of these women were in the lower echelons of their companies, and they rose no higher than middle management level.

When he looked at the changes in the educational levels of women, since nineteen fifty in the USA,
a thought provoking trend emerged.

Women's Share of Total Degrees Earned in the USA from 1950-1985

Earned Degrees	1950 %	1960 %	1970 %	1980 %	1985 %
Bachelor's	23.9	35.3	43.1	49.0	50.7
Master's	29.2	31.5	39.7	49.4	49.9
Doctorates	9.6	10.5	13.3	29.7	34.1
First Professional	n/a	2.7	5.2	24.8	32.8

Source: Men at Risk Prof. Errol Miller compiled from (U.S. Digest of Statistics 1987)

Women have made phenomenal strides in the
twentieth century in terms of their educational
achievements. As early as nineteen–eighty five
(now almost a quarter of a century ago), women
in the US had already begun to outnumber men in
attaining Bachelor degrees.

The percentage changes in terms of professional
degrees, which allow women to enter the workforce at higher levels, were even greater.

Whereas, the Bachelor degrees doubled, the
women started at ground zero in nineteen sixty
(representing only 2.7% of the graduates) with professional qualifications, had increased twelve fold
in a shorter time period, to represent 32.7% of graduates in that level.

This situation is mirrored in our own Caribbean societies. It appears that we, the females in the Caribbean, may even have made greater strides. In nineteen forty eight, when the University College of the West Indies was established, the initial class of medical students already had thirty percent female enrolment. We were already beginning to outstrip the enrolment percentages of the premiere first world countries, as far back as the mid twentieth century.

Rhonda Chapma-Johnson PHD and Joan Vanderpool PHD, in a paper in October 2003, (prepared for the IESAL/UNESCO), presented figures which showed the Barbados Community College projections for female to male enrolment in 2010 and 2011 as being 2.6:1 and 3.2:1 respectively. They further reported an even more startling statistic from the College of the Bahamas, where the projected female to male enrolment for 2010 is a phenomenal 8:1. The anglophone Caribbean remains one of the few areas in the world where females outnumber males in high schools.

Gemma Tang-Nain and Barbara Evelyn Bailey, in their book "Gender Equality in the Caribbean Reality or Illusion 2003", reported a seventy-one percent female enrolment at the Mona Campus of the University of the West Indies. This campus has the highest disparity in male to female registration of all the three University Campuses. Women are thus being equipped to enter the work force at increasingly higher levels. This results in more women being at the helm.

Many women's organizations have been initiated to further the rights of women and to pursue research in women's affairs. One such example is CAFRA (Caribbean Association for Feminist Research). March the seventh is celebrated as 'Women's Day'.

Men on the other hand, having taken for granted their erstwhile position at the top of the totem pole, have not been as quick to explore, or to adapt to, the changing environment in which they exist. Dr. Barry Chevannes and Professor Errol Miller are among the few Caribbean men who are exploring the male female dynamic. Chevannes in the nineteen eighties started a project called Fathers Incorporated. This project was centered on working class men, and sought to deal with the major issues, such as, child support and child rearing.

Men are always slow to explore and to ventilate things emotional, yet the rules of the emotional chess game have long since changed. It is clear that, as the whole, social fabric has changed in the twentieth and twenty-first centuries; females have adapted more and made more fundamental changes than men have made. Hence women have entered the work-force in droves. It has taken some time, but we are occupying increasingly higher levels in the managerial structure of the workforce.

This requires that we become the decision makers. No longer is our role seen as that of taking orders, but rather our role is now to issue them. We juggle three jobs, as mothers/housewives, wives and workers in the workforce. You may note with interest, that I have separated "wife" as a specific job description. Most women find being a wife, a full time job, as they must look after their husbands (their eldest child), as well as managing the children, to whom they have given birth. Men have remained relatively static. In the Caribbean our men have made very little adaptation. It is still the role of the woman to look after the house and the children, while holding down her full time job. The concept of sharing domestic chores is anathema to a red blooded West Indian male.

One of the most fundamental issues, which continues to be the poster boy, for lack of change in the male female dynamic, is the factor of reproduction, and in particular, family planning. For us females in the Caribbean, we still have the absolute indignity of having to get permission from our husbands (legal or common–law), to have a tubal ligation. Men who have had vasectomies are as "rare as hen's teeth", and most have had to be counselled and cajoled, in order to have them consent to the procedure.

If one subscribes to the Darwinian theory of evolution, one might be tempted to posit, that men are
an endangered group, as they are failing to adapt
to this new dispensation in which we exist.

When we combine the failure to adapt, with the
shift in the female position on the workforce totem
pole, and the change in the educational levels of
men and women, we begin to see that there is a
distinct possibility that we are heading for a male
female relationship tsunami.

What evidence do I bring to bear to support my
theory??.....

My evidence comes from the young professional women in their twenties and thirties whom
I encounter in my practice. In the past, women at
their level in this social structure would be eager to
satisfy the societal norms of marriage and children;
in that order. More and more, we see these young
women becoming unmarried mothers. They are ac-
tively looking for a husband, but are failing to find
suitable life partners. Many young men in their age
group are intimidated by their achievements. Under the imperative of their biological clocks, they
opt to have their child.

Many of these young professionals are practicing their own version of eugenics, as they chose the
father to be, based on his IQ, or skin colour, or hair

type, or all of the above. In the Caribbean, where women seek validation of themselves in having a child, these educated women are acting on the one hand in a traditional way, and on the other hand, in a modern way. The unwitting sperm donor may actually be led to believe, that he initiated the chase and that he is the one looking for a little innocuous fling. A phenomenal change in the dynamic is that this woman may opt not to inform her designated sire that the child is his.

Given that many of these professional women travel as a part of their job, they may therefore have, at their disposal, an international group of potential candidates for the potential sperm donor.

Another frame shift, which I have noted, is the number of females who have had proposals of marriage and have turned them down; for one reason or the other. This sub-group, unlike those above, definitely has someone interested in settling down with them. Many are willing to have a child with the man, but not to marry him. She doesn't mind combining his genes with hers, but feels that they do not have enough in common to share their lives. Here again she is practicing eugenics.

If one examines the other side of the debate, we find young men voicing the wish for a 'sugar mama' - a young professional woman who can keep him in the manner which he desires. They are keeping their eyes on the financial horizon. In recent times an increasing number of liaisons, and marriages, are between females whose educational and financial assets, far outweigh those of their male partners.

How does this dynamic of the "kept man" work in a Caribbean society which reveres machismo? Many of these liaisons are short-lived, as the men are persistently taunted by their compatriots.

The statistical report of the Government of St. Lucia, which was last updated in 2001, shows some thirty-two thousand six hundred and thirty-one households in which the status of the male female relationship was not legally solemnized. There were twenty-five thousand eight hundred and fifty three households where the male and female were married to each other. These figures indicate, that in only forty four percent of households, in which a male and female are found, are they married to each other.

In fifty-six percent of the households, where a male and female adult are "regularly" together, they are not in fact married. If we split this fifty six percent into those who actually reside together, and those who have a regular visiting relationship, we see that in only fifty-three (53%) percent of the un-married households, do the males actually reside there. In just over a third of the unmarried house-holds the male is a "ship passing in the night", as the relationship is only on a visiting level. If we then factor in the other statistics, which indicate, that in the two main areas in which children would interface with the public, education (sixty-eight percent) and health (seventy-one point seven percent), women predominate; we begin to wonder where boys find their role models?

The persistent cry, which I hear from women, is that they cannot find men who are willing to settle down and to accept responsibility. The response, I give back, is that the boys have no role model on which to pattern their lives. A boy who has never had the influence of a father in the home, and who has never seen what a father does at home, can hardly be expected to assume the role as an adult. Do we expect him to have a pre-programmed imprint, which shows him how to be a loving and responsible partner?

The role models the boys see portrayed on the television are, in some instances, culturally irrelevant in the Caribbean setting; or in other cases deviant and destructive. The materialistic life styles they see portrayed by their idols in the sports and entertainment arenas create expectations and attitudes, which are not tempered by the wise counsel of a father who guides and moulds. This results in the culture of "fast money", which now exists. Boys are far less likely to "stay the educational course", but are much more likely to drop out of school in the hope of making a "fast buck". Most frightening is the fact that our boy's sense of reality is now more centered around video game characters and their violent acts!!

The statistics from the Government of St. Lucia, show that from the primary school level (fifty-two point seven percent), to the high school level (fifty-eight point eight percent), girls stay the course and have higher academic achievement levels.

Our girls also have a mother on whose life she can pattern her own. She unfortunately, however, lacks a yard stick which she can use to measure the suitability, or unsuitability, of her potential mate; she has had no exposure to what a real man, a caring loving husband and father should be like. Her template shows her that a woman has children, in many instances, from different men. That a woman may practice serial monogamy, and that a woman very often has to raise her children without the assistance of the father. She lacks the learned cues which will help her to choose the right mate.

If we then add into this scenario, the fact that our young girls are being fed a steady diet of video vixens, which use their physical assets as the mainstay of their existence, then we may soon begin to see attrition, even in the educational achievements of our girls.

Our children are also being exposed, at all levels, to alternative life styles; this suggests that the nuclear family may not necessarily mean a female mother, a male father and children. There are thus issues with which the young now have to deal, which the previous generations were spared until they had the intellectual tools to deal with them. I try to process through the mind of a three year old, the current hot topic of the day (in the year two thousand and nine), of "the pregnant man".

These young ones have not yet sorted out their issues with respect to gender and sexuality, and we are already bombarding them with mixed and confusing signals.

I foresee a future which will prove to be complex and difficult for the young. The dizzying array of alternative pairings and family structures will challenge them to find their own pathway to happiness. They will also have to find a sense of themselves, and a sense of acceptance of who they are. It is up to those of us in the older generation to give them the guidance they need. We must lobby to remove the negative influences which swirl around them. It is up to us to provide the moral compass and to lead by example. I do not believe that it is an impossible dream, but I do believe in the immortal words of Dr. Martin Luther King: "The clock of destiny is ticking out, and we must act now, before it is too late."

CHAPTER TEN (10)

"Just Lunch"

THE DATING SCENE OFTEN looks like lots of fun, and perhaps, many of us, especially men, can make a 'sport' out of it.

But what in the world of Business and Human Resource Management, is referred to as "shortlisting the candidates", takes on a whole different dimension when it comes down to, if you like, "short-listing" for yourself, a partner for life.

After all, they come in all shapes, sizes and colours, each with a "tantalizing feature" that the other doesn't have, or at least not to the same degree; so the befuddled bachelor at best, is at first inclined, to perhaps, unknowingly, surround himself with an entourage of possibilities; choices to fit every mood and occasion, but somehow, this still does not satisfy his yearnings.

But, unfortunately for him, the "Laws" (at least in our part of the world), will only allow one <u>legal partner</u> (at a time).

So if and when, he eventually figures out, that he would now settle down, get hitched, hang up his boots, whatever, then he must somehow, 'shortlist', from his many girlfriends, ONE whom he considers has the highest 'compatibility score' with him.

Therein lays one of the biggest decisions of his life, if ever there was one! ...The buck stops with you my friend; it is you, the man, who (traditionally), must propose, it is your judgment call, no one can decide for you, and it is what will be, for the rest of your life!

As alluded to in my earlier observations in this Book, there are agencies set up, to help with the 'shortlisting' process, but that still does not let you off the hook.

Today, professional ladies as well, with their 'high profile' academic qualifications, lifestyles and careers, are facing an equally similar dilemma, and need as much help, with their own "shortlisting of applicants" as their male peers.

So what is it that you look for in the "shortlisting" process of elimination?

As I mentioned, there are "dating agencies" set up in the USA, UK, Canada, (and other larger populated countries of the world), where you could be looking for a 'needle in a haystack' - trying to find that ONE 'compatible' partner; and research is showing, that some "52% of single women and some 48% of single men", are currently using some sort of "dating service", as compared to some 8% back in the 1990's.

Our 'cyberspace' lifestyles with all of its concomitant pressures, no longer permits, to the degree allowed in the past, long walks in the park, visits to the library, going to Church programmes and the like.

Additionally, the new International Security profile of today, also suggests that we might be facing a high risk, just accepting a dinner date, which turns out to be one with some 'psychopath' from out of town!!

I saw an advertisement in a Business magazine, not too long ago, featuring one of the several International dating Service Agencies in the USA, who call themselves "Just Lunch" - apparently founded back in 1991, by Andria McGinty, who, herself apparently, had to deal with a broken engagement; and who suddenly found herself single again,   ('suddenly single' I think the condition is called), and began the idea of the less pressured "Lunch Date".

In 1997 she was joined by one 'Daniel Doland', (a former Harvard Law School Graduate, who had left his career, at one of the blue chip International Law firms in the US), to head up this "Just Lunch" Organisation, which he aptly describes as: "an International Dating Service for busy Professionals".

The upscale dating service, it was said, arranges lunch dates for well educated professionals, in a civilized and discreet manner.

The magazine advertisement I saw went something like this, and I quote: "Singles Scene – You're single, successful and attractive - so why is it so hard to meet that special someone? Believe it or not, out of the 10 million singles currently in the U.S., this is the situation for many of America's best and brightest – busy professionals."

"Enter "It's Just Lunch" a unique dating solution that seems to have smoothed out many of the issues of modern romance."

"The Company was established in Chicago in 1991, after a broken engagement, left its founder "suddenly single", – she then began the tedious search for a way to meet "normal", well-educated professionals. Her friends set her up on blind dates, she tried personal ads, and even thought about a dating service; but wasn't comfortable with any of the options."

THE PERSONAL TOUCH

"The ideal first date", she decided, "was a lunch date." A no-pressure - relaxed situation - where you meet face-to-face, in an environment where you could actually talk. The company's premise is simple: it's a dating solution, based on personalized screening. After a client calls for information, a one-hour meeting is set up, to discuss the type of person they'd like to meet. Generally, within 48 hours, the company calls to tell the client all about their first date. "It's Just Lunch" then arrange for the couple to meet for lunch, or a drink after work, at a restaurant convenient to both of them – they even make the reservations.

Then clients check in with the company and give feedback on the date; before the next one is chosen.

"It's a complete blast" McGinty says. "And I believe there's absolutely somebody for everyone."

If truth be told, The Palm Desert-based company has grown over the past 15 plus years, to be the largest dating service in the world, with over 90 offices world-wide. They are now expanding throughout Europe, Asia and Australia, (in addition to North America), in response to the growing demand for their services. Some of their franchisees were once clients of 'It's Just Lunch'. Talk about believing in the process! Unquote.

Whilst, I have not (personally), had the benefit of their services, from all that they claim, it looks like they know what they are talking about; having carried out their own (scientific) survey, of some 38,912 singles.

Some interesting statistics they came up with was that "79 percent of men on a first date take 15 minutes to determine whether or not, they wish to see the woman again", and that there was a "1 in 8 chance, that a woman has a second date, if she has not heard from him, in 24 hours."

Guys take note, that "64 percent of women, will take an hour on a first date, to determine whether they want to see the man again".

Ladies are therefore infinitely more patient than the "15 minute guy".

Anyway, to find out more, may I suggest you consider contacting them at the advertised number 1-800-300-9500 or visit www.itsjustlunch.com ....

Good luck....

Lets hope my mention of this service is of some use, and the many others, similar in ways to this, which come to mind; example: 'Chemistry.com' or 'E-Harmony' and others, who have taken to the television airwaves, to provide an adequate range of options and choices, for busy professional people, while contributing to their own bottom lines.

While on a recent return visit to my "old" University "in the British Midlands"...ok... England; I was browsing through some of the 'dating' columns of a couple of local newspapers, just to satisfy my own curiosity as to the development of any new and "innovative" ideas that may have arrived on the dating scene; but alas, the level of 'desperation' seems to have intensified even further, since those "College" days back in the late 70's...

Under the headings which targeted "Women seeking men" were a number of 'personal' offerings, which I would attempt to paraphrase for "confidentiality"; never mind that these had already been already published texts...

First in line, there was this "confident dominant female", who knew exactly what she wants - loves to dress up, and desires an older, naughty male, to put in his place!!"...

I wondered who, or how many, guys out there, who would give anything just to be "put in their place?"... guys who accept that they needed straightening out!!...or am I missing the point, somewhere out there in "funland??"

Then there was the "busty black female", with a great bum and long legs (who even specified the length), who wanted a "naughty" older male! .... come on guys ...looks like "naughty" is in...

The "Men seeking Women" columns were a bit more mundane and perhaps more "politically correct", so to speak; with the likes of: "professional male, age '00' seeking attractive, genuine female, to share life with"...

Then there was the more zesty: "77 year old black male, looking for a 69 to 80 year old white lady"....the guys still "got it" man, if you know what I mean?....

In all of this 'confusion' within our Western World, perhaps, there is something to be said for the 'Asian' approach; of the " prearranged parental selection" process, in which the betrothed partners, have little or no say, as to whom they wind up with…But that's for another time…

In any event, what the heck do you do with the "Asian" formula when you're already pushing 60's /70's plus?….parents would have long exempted themselves from such a responsibility…. as they look down from the "pearly gates"(or up), or where ever it is, that we all end up….moving along..

ROMANCE IN PARADISE @ 70's-The "Jade" Experience

Now then, let me share with you what I thought was an interesting and rather "romantic" life experience that I became privy to some time ago.

You see, there was this 'senior' couple who I ran in to, whilst visiting one of the Resorts on the southwest coast of my island home… Saint Lucia.

The couple , then both in their 70's if you like, were vacationing from the UK and were due to be married that very weekend.

For the purpose of 'privacy' lets us 'christen' our couple Bob and Anne; he was seventy seven and she, well, a mere seventy four!

Bob recounts that, "we have known each other from our teens, but it was rather a case back then, of, 'never the twain shall meet'".

According to Bob, he was the "son of a labourer" (nothing wrong with that in my books), and was indeed a labourer himself, working manually on the roads of his hometown; while Anne, on the other hand, was "the daughter of the local Church Minister"... a so called "man of letters", recounts Bob, while my own Dad, "could not even read and write."

Apparently, based on the way "British" societies were structured back then (and possibly even now), that was probably considered "a big deal"... a whole pedigree thing, as the saying goes...

Anyway, somehow, he, (Bob), would find someway of doing his road repair 'work' next to, or nearby, the church where Anne's father ministered; just hoping to catch a glimpse of Anne, as she walked to and from the church.

He was madly in love with "the Ministers daughter", but regarded himself, as, well, "beneath her station in life"; while she (Anne), was quietly curious about a liaison of some sort, but "wouldn't dare" for sake of disapproval by the church flock, and more so, her Pastor Dad.

Years went by, in fact some 60 years went by, during which time, Anne had married 'a chosen one', while Bob tried developing his career and began a Trucking Company; later himself, getting married to someone else ....which apparently put paid to that chapter of their lives.

As he reiterated, it continued to be the case, of, "never the twain shall meet", over the next 60 years ....

Meanwhile, Bob's trucking business grew and grew, becoming one of the largest and most successful in his area; but he always had private thoughts, and 'visions', of the once 'love of his life'; the Minister's daughter Anne, whom he had met and fallen in love with so many "moons ago"...

While his status and income bracket had, over the years, far exceeded what the Minister's family had attained, a 'void' remained which he would have loved to have filled, with his beloved, long since vanished, Anne.

Ah well, by then, Bob must have said... 'Time to move on'... You know the feeling...no point crying over "spilt milk", and all the adages which must have come to mind...

The years rolled by…

By an interesting twist of 'fate', Bob, now in his 70's, was one day part of a group that organized dances for singles at the local "barn" house.

You see, by then, Bob's former wife had 'moved on', as the saying goes, and he was now 'single again'.

Bob had apparently been put in charge of paring couples off for the 'dance-a-thon', with the 'girls one side' and the 'boys on the other' all participants in their 60's, 70's & 80's…

When the music started, the 'girls' would choose a dancing partner and off they would 'whirl away' on the dance floor.

Looks like every one got paired off, except for Bob and Anne, who up to that time, had not even recognized each other.

Bob makes his move over to Anne and says "looks like you're stuck with me!"…

They dance and start talking. "So what's your name? Where are you from? Which family are you from? What do you do?" you know … the usual routine trying to satisfy his curiosity, with the well worn "getting to know you questions" that most 'grown ups' would use, perhaps as their best 'pick up' lines...

To their amazement as they danced, it suddenly dawned on Bob, that this must be the same Minister's daughter with whom he had fallen for in his teens...

"You're name is Anne... daughter of Reverend So and so... from the Methodist Church on Elm Street?"

"Yes, did you know my Dad??"... asks Anne... "You wouldn't believe it but, or perhaps, even remember it"... says Bob... "You remember when you were in your teens, there was some major road repairs going on outside your fathers church? Well, I was one of the workers on that job, just a mere 'labouring' lad, and one day, I came up and said 'hi' to you, and you smiled back at me!"

"Well I don't know what happened, but I fell madly in love with you, and have not been able to get you off my mind ever since then."

'But that was about 60 years ago'... Anne thought out loud... 'Yes, indeed it was... and I have never forgotten it.'

They take a couple more 'twirls' on the dance floor as they probe further. "So where have you been?" Anne asks… "Well, I had been developing a Trucking Business I had started till it outgrew me and so I sold it off and retired…"

"What have you been up to?" responds Bob…. "Well, I was married for about forty (40) or so years, but then my husband died, and so I have been on my own, helping out at the Florists, and the church from time to time."… replied Anne.

"I too was married for a while" says Bob, "but she moved on, to what she considered to be 'greener pastures', and I, well, never remarried."

The rekindling of an 'old flame' was clearly in the making here, as the two swapped stories of their past lives – with Anne, according to Bob, bringing a humorous twist to her stories; which 'sparked' the flame in him even further.

A couple years later, Anne had sold her house and moved into Bob's house, merging their individual assets into a joint 'Pension plan', which they were preparing to share, for the rest of their days.

Their Travel Agent had found them a place in the sun for their wedding, and so, leaving the bleak winter cold behind, in fact, the highest snow fall in about 20 plus years (according to their account); they boarded their transatlantic flight for Saint Lucia, drove to the town of Soufriere and checked in at the award winning "5 Star Diamond Jade Mountain Resort", being part of the 'Anse Chastanet Resort Group'.

The design of this Resort, is, in its own right, an inherent catalyst for the blossoming of romance; with its suites, known as 'sanctuaries', featuring, according to their brochures, "the most spectacular views imaginable of the Pitons and the Caribbean Sea".

The three sided openly designed spaces, with the 4th wall missing, features the bathroom, bedroom and living areas, with infinity edge swimming pool, and 15ft high soaring ceilings; each one flowing into the other, with no formal separations between the sleeping and living spaces.

How's that for an instant "just add water and stir" type of romantic setting?; designed by the mind of a leading Internationally acclaimed architect and owner, Nick Troubetzkoy; utilizing only the best in local stone and wood; and based upon his own philosophy of building in harmony with the Caribbean nature and environment.

With a 360 degree panorama for the 'celestial terrace', at the very top of Jade Mountain, with no TVs, telephones, or radios to distract your attention; with your sanctuary major-domos (butlers), available to unpack your clothes, (if you like), or serve you breakfast in bed, or arrange a candlelight dinner on your balcony; Bob and Anne were set for their wedding, honeymoon and vacation of a lifetime….and you know what I suspect??... The 60 year wait, was well worth it!!…

Now, just how wrong are those of us who think, 'we're too old for romance??'

"No man", as we say down here in the Caribbean, all you need to do, is ensure you've got the "right mix"… just "talk" to my story characters Bob and Anne (and this account is based on a true story of a real life couple in their 70's whom I met personally), for this first hand account.

Even better, why not try visiting their hotel website at (www.jademountainsaintlucia.com) to see for yourself, and no, you can take it from me, that I do not own any shares at Jade Mountain!!…

CHAPTER ELEVEN (11)

Fact or Fiction

NOT TOO LONG AGO, I came across some "bullet points" which, to my mind, were an excellent aid to positive thinking – yes, the sort of mindset, which I suspect, would be a prerequisite, for attaining harmony within oneself.

After all, if an individual, whether male on female, cannot be happy with themselves, happy in their own skin, then there is, I believe, little chance of bringing happiness to another person.

So lets not go around blaming other people for our "dis-ease" – start looking at the glass, as being 'half full' (rather than half empty), and put on a smile within yourself.

Hopefully, you will soon begin to radiate on the outside, what the 'inner side' is feeling.

The inspirational "bullets points" I referred to, can be summarized below as:-

- Focus on what you want, and what you DO NOT want, will disappear.

- You were born, <u>'add value'</u> to the world.

- There is <u>something good</u> about everyone.

- Write down what you appreciate about another person (for example, your spouse).

- You <u>cannot change</u> the other person.

- The <u>power of healing</u> lies within the Human mind.

- Man <u>becomes what he thinks about.</u>

- Disease "(Dis – Ease)", can be turned around, with positive thinking… so say thanks for the (say, cancer), healing in advance.

- There is more than enough to go around (e.g. Joy/Food/Health/Happiness).

- Energy flows where attention goes.

- Visit <u>'www.thesecret.tv'</u>, should you want more.

Switching gears a bit…a well known 'Televange-list', with whom I was honoured to visit sometime in 2008; an inspiring and charming leader indeed, one Pastor Joel Osteen, (of the Lakewood Church in Houston, Texas), admonished, that couples, or singles, whatever the circumstances, "Should not engage in battles that do not matter, battles that they are unable to win."

He went on, that: "Keeping the peace, avoiding a fight, is a greater mark of Honour."

In other words, we should not let our emotions get the greater of us, and say and do things that we later regret, and which keep us from focusing on the things that really matter…this must be good advice, by any measure.

Then there was the, perhaps, more secular, Sherry Dixon, who in an article appearing in one of my home town Newspapers (The Star of December 23rd 2006), set out what she outlines as, "The 12 Rules for Couples", which you may wish to share with your " spouse", perhaps as your next Christmas gift.

The 12 Rules were stated thus………

"On the 12th day of Christmas, my true love gave to me….a sink full of dirty dishes!"

It's not all partridges in pear trees. Christmas can be a testing time for couples, and so she gives you the dos and don'ts, to see you, and your partner, through "the 12 days of Christmas".

"Don't go 'snogging' a colleague at the office Christmas party."

Although some 84 percent of office workers say, they'd be up for it. She says: "Remember you have to face your partner the next day, and the (whole) office on Monday."

Rule #1

Family lawyer Shevelle Wright says: "that in young, childless marriages, the complaint is often adultery at work - this is partly because office parties are becoming weekends, along with nights in hotels," she explains.

Rule #2

"Do put thought into buying your partner a gift. Eddy, age 34, says he is guilty of the typically 'male' Christmas sin. "Like most blokes, I always leave it until the last minute. So I felt terrible when she opened her presents, and by the time she got to the frying pan, she looked really crushed!"

Rule #3

"Don't row over money. Up to 40 percent of us, will put our festive spending on a credit card, and 17 percent, will spend more cash than they can afford this year; according to an Equifax Survey. If you have shared finances, you need to discuss budgets, before they spiral out of control. Decide what kind of Christmas you want and can afford, then stick to it. Is it one present under the tree, or a stocking full?"

Rule #4

"Boys, don't leave all the shopping for your girl-friend."... "I always row with Desmond about what to buy people," says Samantha, aged 25.

   "Whenever I ask him for suggestions, he says: 'I don't care.' Then he questions how much I spend, on every gift."

Rule #5
"The same can be said for household chores, as more than 65 percent of arguments in the home at Christmas, are caused by chores not being done properly. Sixty (60) percent of women say it is more hassle to let their partners cook, because they then have to tidy up after them."

Rule #6
"But equally ladies, don't nag. It's your partner's Christmas too, and apparently, it's not sexy, when we shout with our hands on our hips."

Rule #7
"It's a common one, but try to avoid arguments over whose family you'll spend Christmas with. Your partner may not want to be an extra in your parents 'big affair', but equally 'you' will have to compromise."

Rule #8
"If you are at the "in-laws", be on your best behaviour."... Megan, aged 30, was a little too nervous last year. "I greeted my boyfriend's dad with a kiss on the cheek, but we missed and ending up kissing on the lips. Minutes later, I walked in on his grandmother on the toilet and, for my final performance

of the night, I smashed a crystal glass, that was part of a discontinued set, which had been sent to the family from England."

"Remember, every family has its own rituals and traditions for Christmas. If they want to 'play games', until the Baileys runs out, so be it."

Rule #9
"Don't hark back to old arguments. It's typical to look back over the past year, particularly at the slow times. It can make you wonder what the next year will have in store for you both. Couple, with that, spending lots of time together, it's no wonder many couples end up needing relationship counseling in January."

Rule #10
"This is the season to be 'jolly', but don't get hammered."… "I drank too much white wine at my ex-boyfriend's parents' house last year," says Diane, 35. "I have hazy memories of telling him, his Mum was a control freak, and that his Dad looked down my top."

Rule #11
"Don't act too hastily, if you are feeling stressed. Derek, 35, has ended two relationships before Christmas. 'If things aren't going well, the thought of spending money and effort on someone I'm not that keen on, makes me want to 'bail.' Then there's

the prospect of spending Christmas, with two lots of families and friends."

Rule #12

"Finally, make quality time for each other. The longer you've been together, the smaller this issue becomes. But if you haven't been together for long, you may feel as if you're being cast aside, for relatives and friends. Keep your partner at the centre of it all, as much as you can." Unquote

Fact or fiction you ask…Again I am not going to pretend to be any expert on the subject. But you've got to admit, that there is merit in much of what Ms. Dixon has said to us.

Each 'couple' in my view, should seek to draw on the 'medicine' that best suits your situation, and to quote from Donald Trump, (the US Billionaire Real Estate Magnate) in his book: 'How To Get Rich', his mother, Mary Trump, gave him the 'mother of all advice', when she said to him "Trust in God and be true to yourself."

In other words, at the end of the day, it's all down to you… there is no 'one size fits all' situation, each of us has to deal with our own unique situation, and tailor make the solution to our individual circumstances…

No further comment needed here…

PARENTING AND YOUTH SEXUALITY

With all of this talk of the nuances of gender re-lations, and the world of romance, all of this will invariable result, in a 'family' of some sort; and so I thought we should examine, if only for a moment, a couple of pointers in the process of raising that family.

One of the perennial questions, which emerge from the mind of pre-adolescent youth, is the one which every parent would have to deal with at one stage or another.

"Where do babies come from?" is the question that has jolted many a parent into the realisation, that their 'kid' will need a real answer to, an an-swer which cannot be substituted with 'nonsense' or falsehoods, such as, the 'stork" bringing them and dropping them off; or any of these 'historical-ly' misleading responses.

In the cyberspace world of today, doing so would be at your own peril as a parent, and by extension, creating the potential jeopardy of your child, or children, for their long term future; so I again turn to the experts…

The "1999 World AIDS Campaign", jointly spon-sored by the likes of the WHO/PAHO, the Caribbean Epidemiology Centre (CAREC), the Canadian International Development Agency (CIDA), along with the French and German Technical Cooperation Agencies and the United Kingdom Department for International Development; all got together and put out a simple "Guide for Parents", to assist in dealing with some of the 'transglobal', often innocently, asked questions.

Nicole Joseph, representing the World Aids Campaign, writes, and I quote:

"Our role as parents, elders and caregivers, has become much more challenging and critical. We must therefore, provide our children with:

- Accurate information.

- Honest communication.

- Non-judgmental counsel.

- Complete acceptance, support and respect.

You probably feel uncomfortable talking to your children about sexuality. That's natural. Most adults are not comfortable with their own sexuality and often transmit that to their children unconsciously. Many of us, as kids ourselves, were taught that sex is "dirty" and should not be talked about."

BUT YOUNG PEOPLE ARE NOT SUPPOSED TO BE HAVING SEX!... YOU SAY....

"It's difficult for you as parents, to accept that your children are sexual, or admit that you are, and you are probably afraid to bring up the subject because:

- You think that you don't have the answers.

- You don't know how to communicate about these issues.

- You're just plain embarrassed to talk about it.

What is the big deal anyway?

Children <u>ARE</u> growing up in a different world and, unfortunately, in their world, what they don't know <u>CAN</u> kill them, literally! Gone are the days when the worst things that could happen from having sex, was 'VD' or 'getting pregnant'.

When you don't talk with them, they are very likely to feel, that they can get more reliable information from other sources. Just remember, that most of the values you would like to see in your children, can only be taught by you.

Children and young people <u>WANT</u> to communicate and connect with adults that they trust. They want to have discussions on issues that are important to them for example:

- Their personal relationships.

- Sex and sexuality.

- HIV/AIDS.

and... they want that information to come from you.

It is a fact, that young people make more responsible decisions, when there are caring adults in their lives. They tend to smoke less, or not at all, start having sex later, have less unprotected sex and fewer unwanted pregnancies. It is therefore critical, that you, as a parent, establish a trusting relationship with your children, by talking WITH them and listening TO them."

SO WHAT EXACTLY IS THIS "THING" CALLED SEXUALITY?

Sexuality is not just SEX! We are all sexual, and this includes:

- Our bodies and how they work.

- Whether we are a man or woman.

- Our sexual preferences.

- Our values about life, love and our relationships with others.

WHY DO I NEED TO TALK TO MY CHILDREN?

The latest reports on sexual behaviour among youth, highlight an alarming increase in teenage pregnancies and sexually transmitted infections (STIs), including HIV. Children are having sex at earlier ages, increasing the risks to their health, future, and general well being.

Talking with your children, helps build their trust in you, and makes it easier for you to trust them. It gives them healthy attitudes towards sex and helps to trust them. Most important, talking will ensure that they get correct information and not be misled; by television and movies. Remember, they won't talk to you, if you don't talk to them first.

WHERE DO I START?

Nicole suggests you will, probably, have to bring up the subject. Most probably, your children will not be comfortable approaching you about it, as they might feel that it is disrespectful, or that you might think that they are having sex, and that they might get into trouble with you.

Take them seriously and do not 'tease' or chastise them. Continue to love and support them and let them know that you do. Avoid being judgmental and condescending, otherwise you'll put them on the defensive, and then they won't talk with you, or, even listen to what you say at all.

Put yourself in their shoes. How would you feel if you were treated that way? Understand that communication is a two way process and that you have to listen to them as well.

Listening to them will:

- Let you know how they truly feel and what their concerns are.

- Give them a sense of their importance to you.

- Help to build their levels of self-esteem.

Take advantage of natural opportunities that arise, for example, watching TV or reading the newspaper. Don't pass up opportunities like that. Make sure that you do not bring up the subject, only when there is a problem; that sends the wrong message. Despite what you may think, your children want and need someone to talk to. Who better that you?

HOW DO I PREPARE MYSELF?

- Make sure that you can give correct information.

- Be honest with your child.

- Have a chat with a knowledgeable friend or health care worker.

- Visit the local Family Planning Association.

Be prepared to tell your child, that you will have to look up some information if you need to. But you should always have some important facts up front.

These might include the three ways that HIV could be transmitted:

- Through unprotected vaginal, anal or oral sex.

- Through the exchange of infected blood, such as sharing needles or blood transfusions.

- From an infected mother to her baby during pregnancy, birth or breastfeeding.

Also, if your child finds it easier to talk with another reliable (and here I, as author of this book, would add trusted, repeat trusted) adult… an aunt, uncle, health care provider, priest, pundit, pastor, or imam; don't be offended, encourage it and respect their decision.

WHEN DO I START?

It's a fact, that, young people are starting to have sex at an earlier age, in some cases as early as 12. It is therefore important, to start talking with them before they become sexually active.

Children start learning about sexuality from the time they are born, and you are their best guide.

You need to start, by using the correct names for the parts of their bodies --- your knee, your penis, your vulva, your eyes, your buttocks. You will be teaching them that these are not 'dirty' words.

As your children grow, you will notice that they ask a lot of questions about everything. Don't dismiss or put off answering their questions. This may cause them to seek answers elsewhere and expose them to the myths that are always circulating.

- Be honest and open with your children.

- Where appropriate, talk with them about your own life experiences.

This helps to build trust between you and assures them, that they can talk with you if they have questions. Remember, from the time they go out to school, they will be hearing about sexuality issues. It is up to you as parents, to ensure that they receive the correct information.

At puberty, and in their pre-teens, you might need to work (harder), to keep the lines of communication open.

- Encourage them to ask questions, or come to you with their concerns.

- Ask them questions to find out what they know.

- Talk with them about prevention of disease and pregnancy.

- Let them know that sexual intercourse has serious consequences, for which they might not be prepared.

If you had kept on talking to your child from very young, it will be easy to talk with them about these issues and indeed, about HIV and other STI's.

In their teen years, they are dealing with social pressure from peers and the media. You therefore need to:

- Reinforce the values that you started teaching when they were toddlers.

- Be clear and consistent.

- Provide them with the information and skills to act on those values.

This is also the time, when they would most likely want to start having sex.

- Talk with them about their options.

- Emphasise that abstinence is an option, and is the only sure way, to prevent pregnancy and STI's.

- Talk with them about other sexual activity (such as masturbation), that will not transmit HIV or cause pregnancy.

- Deal with the subject of condoms and other forms of protection and birth control.

- Emphasise that there is time for everything, and that this is the time to concentrate on school, enjoying family and friends, and setting goals.

Remember, children need their parents to help them develop standards and the confidence to make the right decisions. An important point to remember, is, that children learn by example. "Do as I say and not as I do", is not an option!!

How many times did you hear that exact thing as a child? You didn't like it, did you? So don't expect your child to. Examining yourself and changing your own inappropriate behaviour, is a necessary and very important part of the process. Make your actions match your words. You don't want to lose their attention or their respect.

Teach them that sexual responsibility means:

- That not having sex is OK, and is the only 100% guaranteed way, to prevent pregnancy and STI's.

- That responsible partners are honest with each other about their sexual health.

- That responsible partners, discuss, and agree, on protection from pregnancy and STI's at the same time.

- That making responsible choices, increases one's self esteem and self respect.

You owe it to your children to educate and inform them about what they're in for...

- That sex is just one part of a loving committed relationship and requires mutual consent.

- Knowing that sex can have positive and negative consequences, and how those consequences apply to them.

THERE IS NO SUCH THING AS TOO MUCH INFORMATION

Knowing about sex, will not make your children have sex; and not knowing about sex, will not stop them. The more accurate the information that they have, the better they are able to handle the pressures of growing up. Once you get off to the right start, it gets easier for you and your child to be frank, open and honest; and for you to provide clear prevention messages. With your support, they will know that it's OK to say "NO".

If only for your children's sake, endeavour to keep those lines of communication open.

MAKE SURE THAT YOU LISTEN

- Make yourself available to your children, anytime, anyplace.

- Listen to their ideas, their fears, and their dreams.

- Show respect for their ideas, even if you have a different view.

- When they arise, try to solve problems together.

Above all, reassure them, that their sexuality is a natural part of themselves and that their feelings are completely normal. Encourage them to be comfortable with their identity, their feelings and their needs.

Educate them about their rights, and let them know, <u>that they are the only ones</u> who can make decisions about their bodies. Tell them that it is OK to stand up for themselves; and that their rights come with serious responsibilities, of which they must be aware. Again, remember that these messages will not be effective, if you do not 'practice what you preach'.

Yet again, remember that it is easier for children to learn safe behaviours than to unlearn unsafe ones. These are many resources for educating yourself and your children: the Family Planning Association, the nurse, the family doctor, the Ministry/ Department of Health, Library, Non-Governmental Organisations, that deal with health issues, and the internet, are but a few; and it is up to you, to make good use of these resources.

The most important part of teaching your children, about sexuality, is to help them to develop a healthy sense of self.

Respect them, as this shows that they are worthy of respect and valued, and further helps them, to respect themselves.

Assure them also, that while fitting in with their friends is good, that thinking for themselves, and not following the crowd blindly, is more important.

As alluded to earlier in this Chapter, effective parenting is far more challenging today, than ever before in our history, to the extent that you may feel, that you are unequal to the task.

As a result, you need to keep yourself informed about that social conditions and issues, and aware of what is going on in your children's lives. You can no longer take for granted, that they will automatically be safe or well informed.

Yes, just look back and remember the days when our own parents used to, no doubt, 'agonise', with the same questions on dealing with the subject, long before the 'information highway' was invented, and access to the likes of websites and electronic encyclopedia, were ever dreamed of.

Back in those early days, I believe, it was more a question of instilling 'morality' in us. Today, the choice is literally one of survival, one of 'life or death', and so, leaving your child's knowledge of sexuality to chance is just plain 'suicidal'.

So let 'sooner' rather than 'later', be our watch word!

CHAPTER TWELVE (12)

Special Conditions Apply

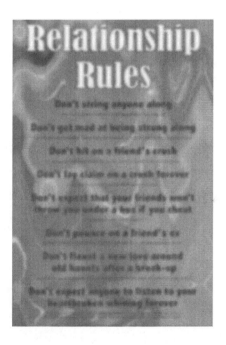

WELL, THE TITLE OF this Chapter, ultimately, became the overall theme and title of this Book "Special Conditions Apply", as it says what all of us have heard, at one time or another, as being the proverbial 'fine print' in any Contract or Agreement.

Prevailing wisdom has always had it, to "let the buyer beware", so you must 'read the fine print carefully'; whether you are buying an airline ticket, a T.V, a toy, a pharmaceutical, or the construction agreement for your home, with the Contractors.

The same is even truer, when we are out in the 'market', for a lifetime partner; someone with whom, we are expected to spend 'the rest of our life'.

After all, in the case of the Ticket, TV, Toy or House, we can always take it back and ask for a refund......

But what if you don't 'read the fine print' of your dating partner's personality, and don't become familiar, with what "Special Conditions Apply?"

The question of taking him/her back and 'asking for a refund' is, to say the least, absurd or ridiculous.

Yes, there are a variety of legal luminaries, Divorce Lawyers and other Mediation experts about, but that is a whole different ball game.

The mere 'emotional bashing' and trauma, associated with 'getting your refund', can be far more costly in cash and/or kind, than you can imagine – in fact, you may well spend the rest of your life, paying to get your 'refund' processed, if you know what I mean!!

The long and short of it is, that the overall object of this Book, is to 'jolt' some reality, some awareness, that, as with any major activity or development in our life, we must 'read the fine' print and the <u>special conditions</u> that apply; 'vetting them carefully', before we simply 'sign up', with the 'hope' of the proverbial ostrich, as he buries his head in the sand.

Yes, the romance, the chemistry, the 'ooh la, la's', and the whatever else you have going, may be fine – and by all means enjoy it, but remember, that sooner or later, there will be a 'day of reckoning', if you take the 'ostrich' route, as alluded to earlier.

A 'microscopic' glance at your mother in law, or father in law to be, should provide useful insight, as to what might be expected later from your significant other; in terms of appearance, personality and 'moral suasion'.

Again, I am not the expert, nor am I pretending to be, I'm just a 'regular Joe', of an ordinary business man, who has needed and, I suspect, still needs, a dose of his own advice!

And so, I set out on this journey, to ask the questions, plant the perspectives and hopefully, prompt a greater level of awareness, of the management principle, of "Let the buyer beware".

FINE EXAMPLE...

I recall in my younger days, my Dad, (who was married to my Mom for over forty five years), always used to make a case, for what he referred to as, the concept of 'Perpetual Courtship'.

He was of the view, that couples after marriage, should 'devise tactics', which would continue to 'trigger' the desire, to see each other, a longing for, a looking forward to, type of pre-marital courtship sort of thing.

To that end, he 'practiced what he preached', and would spend many nights of the week, sleeping in his own bedroom; sleeping in the 'mode', I suppose, as he did before the marriage began.

In fact, I have since discovered, a few 'tactics' of my own, which allow for some semblance of the 'autonomy and independence', that 'bachelorhood' provides; which I venture to list here; for instance....

(I) Instead of buying the large screen (expensive), TV for the living room, you get yourself two smaller TV's ......a 'his and hers' version of a TV set up, which allows 'him' to watch his favourite sports channels, while 'she' has uninterrupted viewing of the Cooking....Home & Garden, Lifetime or Evening News channels; preferably in separate rooms, which then eliminates 'fighting' over the 'control' of a single 'remote control'.

(II) There is much to be said, for sleeping in your own (separate room) sometimes (repeat sometimes), as you get the chance to get some real rest and then to get up and ask caring questions like – 'How was your night', and, 'Did you sleep well?, when you both emerge and head down to the kitchen, to see what's on for, or, to start to cook breakfast.

(III) Couples who live in the same house (yes, standard scenario) and, more so, those who work at the same business place or department, have to be even more innovative, to maintain the principle of 'Perpetual Courtship'.

Devices like meeting for lunch, at a totally neutral spot, has its merits and may even infuse some new content matter into your discussion agenda; which, if otherwise not careful, tends to turn rather monotonous; as common issues of work and home, take their toll.

(IV) The 'dinner and a movie' experience, which may have been routine 'pre-honeymoon', should be re-introduced after marriage, especially those which foster laughter and exhilaration.

I suggest you avoid 'horror' movies, or other forms of 'stressful' entertainment.

Not too long ago, I was reading an article by Nichole Yorio, titled: "What Happy Couples Know", in which she highlights another book, called: "Wonderful Marriage", by Lilo and Gerry Leeds, who had been married for over 56 years (to each other), and in which, they share their wisdom and experience on building and sustaining strong and lasting partnerships.

Among their suggestions included and I quote:

(i) <u>**Be your ideal spouse.**</u> If someone asked you, what you wanted from your partner, you'd quickly rattle off a long list of qualities. But a great relationship starts with you, the couple says: "It's my job to be the kind of partner I want", says Lilo. "I think, '<u>instead of criticizing, what can I do differently</u>?' or,

'What am I doing that is upsetting him?'" Once you commit to improving you, you'll notice a difference in your relationship – and you'll be motivated to improve even more.

(ii) **Think before you speak.** "When I'm angry, I say, 'don't talk to me. I'm busy counting to 100'", Lilo says. "Counting prevents fights from escalating, because by the time I'm done, I either forget why I am mad, or I realize that, what I'm angry about, is unimportant."

(iii) **Ask for what you need, instead of complaining about what is wrong.** If someone bothers you, it's better to get it off your chest, rather than fume. "But there's a big difference between 'we never go out to dinner' and 'I'd like to go out for dinner,'" Lilo says. "Asking, sets a positive tone, and is more likely to get results."

(iv) **Make your marriage a lifelong courtship.** "Just because the honeymoon ends, doesn't mean the romance has to stop," Lilo says. Gerry adds, "We are still holding hands, making love and sking down mountains together – we knew we would be happy, when we met, more than five decades ago, but the reality is better than our dreams"… Unquote.

Again, as part of my Research on the subject matter of this Book, I came across yet another article, by Redbook Publication House, of their Publication titled: "500 Great Dates", (With tons of fun plans), which I believe, seems to supports the notion I have been advancing, based on my Dads model of 'perpetual courtship'.

The Book writers posit the angle, that, "You'd think by the time you're a couple, and possibly have a child, or three, under your belt; you'd be able to handle the intricacies, of going out for the night with your man. After all, that was part of the allure, of the going from 'me' to 'we'. You were finally able to leave the whole dating game, and it's so- called 'rules' behind."

But, dating for <u>long-term</u> couples, comes with its own new 'his-and-hers' matching set of pressures, especially when kids are in the picture. You no longer have the time, to make sure you have five minutes together, without interruption; let alone set aside an entire evening, to dote on each other. So when the stars are finally aligned – you've cleared your calendars, you've found someone, not featured on televisions "Most Wanted" list, to look after the kids – you want the evening to be perfect, which practically begs, for a "Murphy's Law" moment.

"Don't sweat it" they say, "You can lay the foundation, for lots of fun nights out (or in), by following simple save-the-dates guidelines. First, make sure that at least every other date, gets you out of the house, and away from your daily life. Second, be clear about who is doing what planning-wise, or you may end up doing nothing. Finally, take turns organising your dates. So what if he has no clue, which 'restaurant' got the best review? This isn't about planning the perfect evening; it's about having time with the person you love, so you can rediscover, talk, laugh, and enjoy each other."

Redbook have therefore come up with what they describe, as, "43 ways to do just that", some, of which, are listed below for your preliminary digestion, but I would suggest, you consider getting their "500 Great Dates" book, for the full picture.

Again I quote from their "dinner and a movie done" better suggestions:

Upgrade the Saturday-night standard, with these following tips:

Turn your night into a "mini-vacation", by matching the menu to the movie: Kung Fu action flick? Order some spicy noodles at your local Chinese restaurant. French film noir? Hit the nearest bistro, Italian family drama? Share a big bowl of spaghetti… (You can create your own combinations), and may, I add, the "Caribbean equivalents"…lest we forget!!…

Now! Choose a restaurant that has small tables, or ask to sit side by side; so that you can't help, but "rub knees.

Try brunch and a matinee: Your neighbour-hood's fancier restaurants are way more affordable (and just as delicious), in the daytime hours.

Find a restaurant with a dance floor. Even if you've got less co-ordination, than a "Dancing with the stars" early-round reject, you can still hold each other close, and sway to the beat.

Laugh like a kid again, at the latest 'G or PG' rated movie. "It makes me laugh to watch him giggling like some 7-year-old", says one woman who regularly goes to children's movies with their husband. "It reminds me of why I fell in love with him: his silly, fun side." Get enough animat-ed fare in your daily life? Skip "Shrek the third", and chuckle over the infectious goofy humour, or whatever Farrelly brothers or Ben Stiller 'flick', is on offer.

Create your own 'drive-in' experience. If you have a laptop with a DVD drive, take it out with you. Rent or download a movie, you never got around to seeing, order something simple, at a 'dimly lit' bistro, find a love seat to cuddle up in, and watch. From it's 'Instant Watching' library of 1,000 films, Netflix's (USA), most popular DVD-rental plan, now lets users access movies (up to 18 hours' worth a month), which can be 'zapped' straight to a PC in seconds. Another option: (for around $20 a month), you can get a software, that will let you download a wide assortment of movies, (go check out cinemanow.com and movielink. com), or again, guys, the Caribbean equivalents.

CHEAP DATES!

Redbook goes on to recommend, that you "Give yourselves the 'VIP treatment', without the expensive price tag!"

"Go for an all-day hike (persons based in the US, can check out <u>trails.com</u>, for a listing of nearby treks), and get lost in the woods together."

In the Caribbean, with our twelve months of summer, there is no end of possibilities – you can touch base with your local National Trust or Naturalists Societies Calendar. Again in the Caribbean, we have 'Creole Day (Juonen Creole), River Limes (picnics), Rain Forests and an abundance of Water-falls, Beaches and other great escapes.

Then go 'sip some fine wine'. Find out if your local wine or 'liquor' store, hosts tasting nights. It only becomes expensive if and when you buy! Other specialty stores often hold tastings too. Check out chocolate stores, cheese shops, or ethnic-food markets.

Hit the Gym...Get 'sweaty' together. It'll feel less like a chore, and more like a 'we're-in-this-to-gether' moment; when you help each other to get hearts pumping and cheer each other along. What about trying couples yoga, or a Spa?... or twisting your body, into a pretzel pose, bringing you closer together in everyway.

Visit the Museum. (Museumstuff.com has links to thousands of art institutions in America and abroad; the Art Museum Network at amn.org lists links to the Websites, and exhibition calendars of the world's leading art museums; and galleryguide.org will help you easily locate an art venue near you).

Again, the local National Trust, has its array of historical displays, and even "animation centres".

If art really isn't your (or his) thing, don't over-look other kinds of exhibits; such as the history of hockey, or even, surgical equipment! One good source for the weird and wild: museumspot.com. Ok, you get the gist of it – go find your local equivalent and be creative; I should again, also, put in a plug, for the St. Lucia National Trust Museum at Pigeon Island, the Desmond Skeete Animation Centre, at La Place Carenage, and locations elsewhere on my home island - St. Lucia.

Again according to Redbook, safety permitting, you can "Go camping overnight - There's no TV to interrupt your conversation, and the night is long, so you can retire early to your sleeping bags (zipped together, of course)".

Redbook go on to suggest, that you spend an afternoon test-driving cars, viewing model homes, or store window-shopping. Even if you have no interest in making a purchase now, these activities can kick-start discussions about your goals. New lovers are always dreaming together, about the things they want to achieve: exotic trips, houses, and children.

As love matures, you become more focused on the here and now – attending school meetings, folding socks – and forget to write the next chapter of your own love story; or think you don't have to, because you've already discussed it all before. But continually setting shared goals, gives love something to work towards, and shape itself around.

Give in to the undeniably romantic allure, of watching the sun go down. Head to the highest point in town, and when the light is 'romance-perfect' for enhancing your sensuous mood, turn the scenic view into the background for a make-out session.

My Caribbean equivalent, if I might suggest, is searching for the "Green Flash" at sunset – a unique metrological phenomenon, where you keep your eyes peeled, until the sun gently descends behind the horizon, and 'suddenly', an amazing glow or 'flash of green light' can be seen (on a clear cloud free day) – Give it a try…At best, it can be a good 'excuse' to go back to the 'mountain' together!

Work with me here guys…

ROMANCE EACH OTHER

Still drawing on the Redbook recommendations; try to reconnect with these 'so-sweet' ideas…

Relive your first date. Follow the same itinerary and include as many of the original details as possible. Even though <u>you know</u>, how the night will end this time around; recalling how you talked, explored, and began your lifelong journey of getting to know each other, can remind you, that there is still much to learn about yourselves and your relationship.

Have a gourmet style picnic. Cruise the aisles of your local favourite Supermarket and load your cart, with whatever epicurean delights you can find: lobster salad, good-quality chocolate, wine or fizzy grape juice, gourmet crackers, gooey cheeses, and so on. Hey! What ever you can afford!

Now! Head for the most romantic spot in town. If it's too hot, cold (rainy), or wet, to eat alfresco; why not try the atrium at the local zoo, (if you have one), botanical gardens, Museum, or Mall?

Get decked out – even if you're just going to the loc0al diner. Slip into your most glamorous 'duds' – and have him do the same. No matter where you go, looking like your best version of yourself' will make the evening feel special, and inspire connection (and passion).

Take a dance lesson, even if you end up, stepping on each other's toes; you'll be forced to pay attention to how your bodies move together. Avoid dances that do not involve touching. Instead, try learning how to: reggae, calypso, tango, waltz, or even square-dance. At the end of the lesson, be prepared for your dancing partner, to sweep you off your feet and straight into bed – If that is what you had fantasised, of course!

How about renting a rowboat, for a DIY sunset cruise and dinner? (For non tropical residents, keep your drinks cold, by tying a rope around the bottle neck, or using a net to carry it, and trailing it behind you in the water). Pack a blanket, lie back, and wait for the stars to appear. Don't forget to make a wish together, on the first one you see.

Go see a fortune-teller (?) It doesn't matter if she gets it right. (Do you really need a crystal ball, to tell you that you were meant to be?) But it can be a giggle (if she's wrong), or inspiring (if she's in the ball-park), to hear how a stranger reads your romance.

Have a picture-perfect night. Take a camera with you and at different points on your night out, ask people to take your photo (make it a point to 'lock lips' for some snaps). On your next date, flip through the photos together – or make a collage or slide show". Unquote.

The list as I mentioned earlier, goes on, but if you want more, 'fair is fair' – go buy Redbooks Book!

Personally, as your writer, I would add to the long list of ideas and suggestions, that you consider a Cruise on one of the larger Cruise lines, like Royal Caribbean, Princess Cruises, Holland America, Cunard, Celebrity; who all offer excellent packages; and with more and more Cruise Ships being constructed each year, the choices from the Caribbean, to Alaska, to the Mediterranean, are virtually unlimited, and becoming increasingly affordable.

In some of my personal research readings, I came across the, perhaps, 'controversial' statement, on the supposed fundamental difference between women and men, that went: "A woman wants <u>one man</u>, to satisfy her <u>every need</u>", while on the other hand "A man needs <u>every woman</u>, to satisfy his <u>one need</u>" (?)

Not sure, who the original author of that thought was, but as I wind down in my writings, I suspect there is some 'wisdom' in there somewhere; and if only to create awareness, that there is a difference in the psychological 'DNA' of the two genders, which 'kicks in' at about puberty.

My psychological Theory that "Women carry an 'Instead of' DNA", while men on the other hand, carry the "<u>All inclusive</u>"(as well), DNA; I believe has merit, as we seek to decipher the nuances of male/ female interaction, whether as a 'sport', or other- wise, intended to result, in life long marital bliss.

Simply put, the conflict seems to stem from the instinctive variances, in the perspective of males and females.

In my humble view, the whole dilemma can be reduced to just two words on either side of the gen- der divide

The female…"<u>Instead of</u>"… versus… the male… "<u>As well</u>".

Malcolm A.J. Charles

To begin to gain an existential appreciation of ourselves, is to begin to understand, the perspective that we bring to the 'debate' between the sexes.

Bearing in mind that at the end of the day, it is down to us how we perceive ourselves and the partner with whom we choose to share life's space with in the future.

So, in my opinion, knowing what <u>questions</u> to ask ourselves, I believe, is the 'quintessential' first step, to finding the answer to the harmony we all secretly or overtly seek.

In relationships, it is said, that "A soft answer turns away wrath", which is similar in context, to another saying, that "Money will buy a fine dog, but only kindness, will make him wag his tail."

Again in my readings sometime ago, was an illustration of how men might begin to perceive and understand their women partners.

Women, it was said, tend to be, 'multipliers' of whatever is given to them – ergo, "If you give her a house, she will make it a home; if she gets your sperm, she will produce a baby; if she gets groceries, she will produce a meal; and so my friends, if you give her hell, you can expect some serious hell fire in return."

The idea therefore, is to be well meaning and honest with each other – forget the confrontational models, of the so called relationships that we often see on TV sitcoms.

There are two sides to every story and these sides could both be right (as well as wrong), depending on the 'latitude' you perceive them from.

Tell your man, or your woman, what it is exactly that you like or dislike, and don't just assume that they know; nor do I mean tell them only when in the midst of a 'heated argument', you know what the "acronym" called "assume" means ?…yes "AS-SUME"… never assume, because it only makes an "ASS - out of -U- and- ME!!"

So be sensitive my friends and remember, in all that we do, read the fine print, as invariably you will find, that "Special Conditions Apply."

Au revoir…..

BIBLIOGRAPHY

(i) Internet Humour –various (international)

(ii) National News papers (Voice & Star Publishing Co– St. Lucia)

(iii) Jill Adler – Wifes Bill of Rights (USA)

(iv) Craig Playstead – Husbands Bill of Rights (USA)

(v) Dr Marie Grandson-Didier –Consultant Physician & Dermatologist

(vi) Andria Mc Ginty & Daniel Doland-"Its Just Lunch" – USA

(vii) Redbook Publications International - USA

(viii) Pastor Joel Osteen – Lakewood Church, Houston, Texas – USA

(viiii) Nicole Yorio & Lilo & Gerry Leeds – USA

(x) Sarah Peter – Youth Oriented Magazine – Voice Pub Co. St. Lucia

(xi) Pastor Dr John Hagee – Cornerstone Church –Texas, USA

(xii) Steve Calechaman – Men's Health Publications – USA

(xiii) Donald Trump – How to Get Rich – Random House – USA

Chapter 9 References

- Buckingham G. et al Visual Adaptation to masculine and feminine faces Influences generalised preferences and perceptions of Trustworthiness Evolution and Human Behaviour 27 (2006) 381-389

- Chapman-Johnson PhD and Vanderpool J.Phd. IESAL/UNESCO October 2003

- Desnoes Richard - The Dark Side of the Bleaching and Browning syndrome

- Durante Kristina- Ass. Prof. Proceedings of the Royal Society of London Biology Letters Jan. 2009

- Miller Errol - Men at Risk Jamaica Publishing House Ltd. 1995

- Newswire -The Rockefeller University Science for the benefit of Humanity - Nature On Line Sept. 2007

- Parker Randall -August 2008 University of Liverpool/University of Newcastle

- Pipitone N. Gallup G. State University of New York at Albany evolhumbehav.2008.02.001

- St. Lucia Vital Statistics Report 2001- www. stats.lc.gov

- Tang-Nain G. / Evelyn-Bailey B. -Gender Equality in the Caribbean Reality or Illusion 2003

- Whelan Christine/Christine Boxer - Mate Preference survey 2008/ University Iowa-USA

AUTHORS PROFILE

Malcolm Arthur John Charles was born on the Caribbean island of Saint Lucia, and has had a life long love for poetry, writing and music from ever since he was a child, spending much of his spare time at High School, playing the piano and organ, writing songs, poetry and short stories, which he shared among his closest friends and family.

Having finally begun publishing some of his work at the turn of the new millennium, he today continues writing as his hobby, which he regards as diversion from the stresses and strains of life, in his role as a Certified Business Management professional, Corporate Development Consultant and an active Community Service Volunteer with various humanitarian organisations, including the St. Lucia Rotary Club, for some thirty years.

Today, he attempts to take on a somewhat 'taboo' subject of adult relationships, in an attempt to raise knowledge and awareness of the similarities, and more importantly, the differences between the genders; absence of which, have sat at the heart of potential conflicts in private and personal adult relationships, and the concomitant erosion, by extension, of economic and national productivity, in the wider business community.

A UK Business Management Graduate and Justice of the Peace (JP) since the early 1990's, he is a member of the Poetry Society of the United Kingdom, and was bestowed in the Queens Birthday Honours, as an Officer of the British Empire (OBE), for services to the local business community and that of the wider Eastern Caribbean.